IMAD S. ENCHASSI

CLOUD
MILES

*A Remarkable Journey of
Mercy, Peace, and Purpose*

© 2020
Published in the United States by Nurturing Faith Inc., Macon GA,
www.nurturingfaith.net.

Library of Congress Cataloging-in-Publication Data is available.

ISBN: 978-1-63528-090-6

Lani R. Habrock, editor

DEDICATION

To all the women in my life who made me the man I am today:
Especially my mom, Nematt Ades,
who taught me that love is unconditional
To my teacher, Ms. Samira Abou Rahma,
who instilled in me that mercy has no religion and no borders
To my wife, Judith Aguilar,
who believed in me when people doubted me;
who accepted me when everyone rejected me;
who consoled me when people attacked me;
who supported me when people opposed me

To my family:
Especially my father, Said Enchassi,
who was always looking for home
To my siblings, specifically my brother, Assaad Enchassi,
who found me a home in America

To my friends, teachers, and in particular
the interfaith community who made me
unapologetically Muslim, unapologetically Palestinian,
unapologetically American, and unapologetically human

CONTENTS

FOREWORD

Both of my parents were Holocaust survivors. Never once in their lifetime did I hear them use the word "hate." In my almost 20 years knowing Imad, as a colleague and more importantly as a friend, never once have I heard him utter that word either. *Cloud Miles* shows that we must focus on compassion, healing, and mercy.

At 17, Imad volunteered as a White Helmet during the civil war in Lebanon, helping the severely injured in the midst of unspeakable horrors, never asking what religion they were. His description of the massacre is haunting. Yet, in spite of seeing man's inhumanity to man, Imad still believes in the goodness of people. He draws from his own tenacity, strength, and courage to help others.

Imad was helped as a refugee in Lebanon by Samira Rahma, a Catholic nun, whose name translates to "mercy." Through her kindness, generosity and grace, he developed an undiminished capacity for mercy. One example not mentioned in the book is that each year, for more than a month at a time, he and his wife, Judith, travel to Lebanon and Syria to help refugees. And just as Samira Rahma would always give him sugar candies, Imad takes sugar candies to pass out to the refugee children.

When the swastikas and racist comments were painted outside of the Oklahoma Democratic headquarters, Imad was among the first to arrive. He made calls to local interfaith volunteers to come help clean it away. Instead of complaining, he focused on serving the community.

To anyone seeking to understand the importance of interfaith work of building bridges of love and understanding, I wholeheartedly recommend *Cloud Miles*. In this time of incivility in our country, this book is needed more than ever.

I was recently asked what gives me hope. I answered with two words: "Imad Enchassi." This book personifies the reason I gave that answer.

Michael Korenblit
President and Co-Founder
Respect Diversity Foundation

ACKNOWLEDGMENT

This book could not have been written without the skill
and dedication of Lani R. Habrock, who helped me
tell my story in both fact and poetry.

INTRODUCTION

Planes rumble when they take off. They jolt and bounce your insides like water in a balloon. My insides already felt like water. I had been back home to Palestine many times before, but never like this.

Like the pope, I had always entered Israel via Jordan. But this time, with a handful of Christian clergy and two rabbis, I would be flying in through Ben-Gurion Airport. Our group took up an entire section of the plane—at least six rows on the left side facing the cockpit.

I looked out the window and watched the wing cut through clouds. We were speeding through hundreds of clouds per minute. I started calculating speed per "cloud minute" in an attempt to keep my thoughts calm. I wondered how it would feel to set my feet on the grounds claimed by Ben-Gurion.

Would it feel like a betrayal? How many of my own people would see me as a sellout? Would it, in some way, feel like healing?

I was also worried about security. I am always "randomly" selected for additional security screenings and interrogations. I have started joking that my name is "Mr. Random." On this trip, especially, I was prepared to be held up.

Already, even while still on American soil at Newark Liberty Airport, I had experienced two separate sets of screening: once through baggage with everyone else, and then again on the way to our gate to board for Tel Aviv. This latter screening was done by Israeli security.

The first time I entered Israel, through Jordan, I was interrogated by Israeli security in a room decorated with Qur'anic scripture and verses of Hadith (the written oral tradition of the Prophet Muhammed) painted in Arabic on the walls. These were all verses reminding the Muslim visitor of the virtues of telling the truth. This was the early 2000s—before social media was widely used. They knew everything about me.

After sitting in the room by myself for several minutes, Israeli agents entered the room to ask their questions. They knew everything about me. They knew I was active in my community and that I attended mosque regularly. They knew my ancestors and that I was from a formerly wealthy family. When they asked why I was crossing the border, I told them to visit my aunt.

They then showed me four pictures and asked me to identify which one was my aunt. They asked if I had my Lebanese-Palestinian refugee ID with me. I did not. I was an American citizen by then and only had my passport. They then produced a copy of my ID. The sheer amount of information they had on me was unsettling, and I could tell this was their intention—to unsettle me by showing me they knew everything.

When I became an imam, it got much worse. They would ask what kind of sermons I give and if I give anti-Semitic messages. They knew of an incident of someone with ISIS threatening me, which I had reported to the FBI. I had told no one of this. My wife did not even know, as I didn't want her to worry.

Now, years later, the Israeli agent interrogating me knew of this occurrence and many other private details. All the while, I was sitting there stripped down to my underwear. Thinking of this, I was having anxiety thinking of how, if the group waits for me, they will no doubt miss most if not all the tours and destinations scheduled for the first day.

Finally boarding the flight, I sat down next to the window. I watched New Jersey disappear behind a sea of mist. My wife of 25 years sat next to me, leafing through a magazine. Many women, like my wife, were wearing head coverings, but they were not all Muslim. Many were Orthodox Jews.

As a Muslim, I pray five times a day. And often on long flights, prayer time falls while I am in the air. When this happens, I typically do my prayers discreetly in my seat, pretending I am yawning or stretching. On this flight, however, I was comfortable being open with my praying. Orthodox Jews pray three times a day, and their prayers on this flight coincided with mine, so I found myself in a corner of the plane prostrating and praying with my fellow Jewish travelers.

It felt like I was supposed to be doing this trip. It felt purposeful, and perhaps mandated by God. I was going back home, yet as a visitor. I was like a bird returning to its nest, only to find a new family moved in and my memory was forgotten.

I was viscerally aware of my overlapping identities. I am a Palestinian Arab, raised with the narrative that Jews and Israelis are the enemy of my people and not to be engaged with in discourse. I am Muslim and an imam who holds every word of the Qur'an in my brain and spirit. I have verses seared into my consciousness telling me to respect and dialogue with those following the Abrahamic traditions. These are "people of the book," and we worship the same God.

> *We have believed in Allah [God] and what has been revealed to us and what has been revealed to Abraham and Ishmael and Isaac and Jacob and the Descendants and what was given to Moses and Jesus and what was given to the prophets from their Lord. We make no distinction between any of them, and we are Muslims [in submission] to Him.* (Qur'an 2:136)

> *We believe in that which has been revealed to us and to you [Jews and Christians] and our God and your God is the same.* (Qur'an 29:46)

These verses played through my head as I stood praying next to the Jews accompanying me on this flight.

I am an American. This identity is deeply sacred to me because this is the one I chose. I am an immigrant who fell in love with Lady Liberty and ran to her shores, leaving everything and everyone I knew and cherished behind, just so I could have this identity, so I could hold this blue passport in my hand. I am seen as a traitor by some for having this citizenship.

All three identities of my being struggle against one another. I am canvas stretched over frame. But these quarrelling parts cannot be separated. Perhaps on this trip, I thought, they will find peace with one another.

There are so many lines drawn by humankind to define each other. Yet I am crossing them all, one cloud mile at a time.

CHAPTER 1

Trail of Tears

My refugee camp was densely populated, with sewage running through the streets, the ever-present sound of life barely stolen from the hand of death, and the smell of humans mixing together. It was home for the homeless.

Lebanon is located along the eastern Mediterranean shore. It is bound to the north and east by Syria and borders Israel (or Palestine, to my father) to its south. It was an important port of trade between east and west. The ancient people living there called their land Canaan and were known by the Greeks as the Phoenicians.

They were lauded for their seafaring skills, founding colonies throughout the Mediterranean—including Cyprus, Crete, and Carthage. They established trade routes to Europe and western Asia and circumnavigated Africa a full thousand years before the Portuguese. Lebanon is also known for its trees. Beyond the coastal lands are mountainous regions with thick forests of cedar. The cedars of Lebanon are thought to be what made the cross of Jesus. Today there are pilgrimages made to a tree known as the "mother tree" that many Christians visit every year. Solomon's temple was also said to have been made of the cedars of Lebanon.

These rugged terrains have served throughout history as a place of refuge for those seeking asylum from religious and political oppression. Thus, it is today the most religiously diverse country in the Middle East. It is estimated that a little under 60 percent of the current population is Muslim. Islam is sharply divided theologically between Shia and Sunni. The Muslim population in Lebanon is divided almost exactly in half between the two, which is not the case for the greater Muslim world, with roughly 90 percent of the Islamic population identifying as Sunni.

Before 1920, Lebanon was part of the vast Ottoman Empire. After World War I, Western Europe divvied up the Middle East, implementing government systems and leaders without understanding the political and social issues of the territories. Thus, the Middle East became the volatile region it is now. Lebanon was cut out of Syria and given to the French as an independent state. In 1926, the Lebanese constitution was drawn up.

This political system, which continues to guide Lebanon's government, is deeply entrenched in religion.

The French continued to preside over Lebanon until midway through World War II. In 1943, France agreed to transfer power to the Lebanese government. And this brings us to 1948, the establishment of Israel, and my family's flight to Lebanon for asylum.

My father grew up in a wealthy family in Jaffa, Palestine. The Enchassi family owned many businesses and properties. My grandmother was a queen, attended to by the adoring eyes of my grandfather and household servants. Her life had been one of glamour and petting. But wealth can be fleeting, as was this former life she never spoke about.

I can only imagine that this loss was too great for her to bear. It closed in around her and swallowed her whole. She became an imprisoned queen—trapped in the ghetto of Sabra and Shatila. When I knew her, she would never leave her room. Her despair was as thick as the concrete walls of our house.

My grandfather never gave up hope. He lived as a refugee from 1948 until his death in 1963. Throughout those 15 years, not a day went by that he didn't listen to the news on the radio and say, "We are going back soon." Like Homer's *Odysseus*, my grandfather longed for his home.

He orchestrated his time in Lebanon as though it were temporary—never settling in, never planning to spend the next day outside of Palestine. My father said my grandfather died of a broken heart.

It's easy to not feel at home there. It's easy to live as my grandfather did, as though you are laid over in an airport between flights, waiting for your real destination. Every few years there would be an uprising or talk of an Arab nation invading Israel. Each time, my father and grandfather would stand to catch their delayed flight.

They would pace, expecting this time to be the time they left the tarmac. The pacing would turn to awkward, aimless wandering. Small talk among neighbors would resume, and we would all go back to the normal, restless waiting of refugees—living off fast food and trinkets from our carry-on bags.

Growing up, my father told many stories about his life in Jaffa. He used to show me the deeds to my grandfather's properties, the house keys that were kept in tin cans. He used to draw on sheets of paper the layout of his home, after decades still remembering every detail. As if he was ashamed of his refugee life, he would compare our house to the one he grew up in.

Our couch was ugly, but the furniture his father had was beautiful, soft, ornate, and made by the best craftsmen. Our house in Sabra was small and filled with many family members, but our home in Palestine was expansive with vast rooms for each of us. In Sabra we were surrounded by concrete walls, but in Palestine our home overlooked the sea in careless freedom.

In Lebanon we were servants, but in Palestine we had servants. My father spoke of how his father traveled a lot for business and for pleasure. I listened to this wide-eyed. In Sabra and Shatila, we could not leave. The city had invisible lines drawn through it, dividing Christians from Muslims, and to cross them meant detainment—or worse.

I never knew Palestine as home, but I felt it in my bones, saw it in the head my father held high, and heard it on his tongue. His past life felt like my own memories. I repeated his stories to my friends. I saw myself living another life in an alternate universe, like looking into a mirage.

It was just out of reach. This other life was just real enough to see in all its vivid colors, but not enough to hold on to. Yet, these stories formed my identity and seeded a hope that I, too, could someday be more than a refugee.

In Arab culture, family name is a big thing. My father's stories gave me a sense of pride in my family name and made me feel that we should live up to the great accomplishments of my grandfather and his fathers before him, despite our meager accommodations.

Life in Sabra and Shatila was divided like Indians and cowboys. We watched black-and-white rivalries through rabbit-eared antennae. My cousins had a television we loved to watch when we had the chance. It was an escape from poverty and rejection, as I imagine television is for many people. But as refugees, it was a window into a world that existed beyond the walls that imprisoned us in a life of poverty and hunger.

We imitated spaghetti westerns and imagined what life in America would be like. "Cowboys and Indians" was our favorite game. My family history would have had me in the role of an Indian, but no one ever wants to see himself as the loser.

Malcolm X said, "If you are not careful, the newspapers will have you hating the people who are being oppressed and loving the people who are doing the oppressing." Like this, I identified as a cowboy and had fun pretending I was more important than the scruffy kid wearing his brother's hand-me-down clothes I saw in the mirror.

I can now see that the "games" we played as children were tragic, games that started at the sound of sirens. First, we would hear the bombs sailing through the air. Everyone could identify the distinct sound of incoming versus outgoing missiles. Then the "cool" kids—the older, braver, and smarter kids we looked up to—would showcase their expertise by telling us how big the last bomb was and what kind they knew it to be based on the sound.

After the banging and the shaking, we would emerge from under tables and desks or whatever shelter could be found on a moment's notice, and go looking for pieces of shrapnel we called "toys." The kid who picked up the most was the hero, a peer to be envied.

One time, crouched down and locked in my mother's embrace, we listened to the abating sounds of outgoing bombs. "I hope it kills them all," I said to her. "You hope it kills who?" she scolded with a harshness I was not used to. "Other children like you on the other side? Mothers like me?"

I squeezed my eyes shut under the folds of her clothing, trying not to weep.

PALESTINIAN TEARS

If you had seen my family 30 years before my birth, you could never have imagined the horrors we would experience in the span of one generation.

In Palestine, my grandfather, Assad Enchassi, was known for being a charitable man. He owned many properties throughout the region and gave generously and indiscriminately. His charity also extended to funding the freedom fighters combating British occupation. This was, of course, a losing cause.

During British colonization when the persecution of the Jewish people by Hitler began, many Jews fled to Palestine for safety. My grandfather had compassion for the persecuted and allowed Jewish refugees to live in his apartments free of rent.

He also owned a slaughterhouse and was one of a few Muslims who carried kosher meats to accommodate religious dietary needs. During this time, the Jewish population swelled from 3 percent to 20 percent. The bitter pushing and tearing of war were turning the world on its axis, but Palestine, and my grandfather, had yet to feel the fallout.

Many people say the Israeli-Palestinian conflict is thousands of years old, rooted in theological differences and endemically unsolvable. During the 600-year reign of the Ottoman Empire, however, Jews, Christians, and Muslims lived in peace in Palestine. Unrest in the region is only as old as my grandfather's generation.

For 400 years, Palestine had been under Ottoman rule, but in 1917, during the First World War, Britain issued the Balfour Declaration in support of a Jewish state being established in Palestine. The Jewish population at this time was a very small minority. This was the beginning of the end of Palestine as we knew it. From there, Zionism, fed by the fat of the West, grew until it swallowed us.

Nearly two decades later, the declaration caused one of the largest strikes in history, lasting six months. In response to this, the British arrested 800 Palestinians and destroyed their homes. More than 200 family homes were demolished in Great Britain's swift punishment.

My father's home in Jaffa was an Ottoman-style palace with a large entrance opening up to a courtyard abounding in fig, olive, and pomegranate trees and grape vines. The glory of the garden was a Turkish fountain made of marble and mosaic. As a little boy, my father could often be found floating in the fountain without a care and totally nude.

The courtyard led to a large open living area, which broke off into several rooms and a kitchen. The house was three stories tall with a basement, and the top floor sported a luscious balcony garden with potted shrubs and plenty of outdoor seating. This is where my grandparents would throw parties.

In Palestinian culture, it is customary for the elder of the group to lead conversation. In my family, this would have been my grandmother, and she was good at it. She was spirited and genteel. She knew the rules of etiquette and possessed great competence in the skill of conversation. She loved to host gatherings, formal and casual. During these events she was most in her element.

These parties lasted through the evening and into the furthest reaches of the night. Sometimes there would be music. There was always hookah. Neighbors would bring cakes, sweets, and nuts—anything to keep the conversation going.

My father would fall asleep outside in the open breeze of the balcony, swaddled in the quiet hum of dusk-laden discussions, and would wake in his bed. Friends and family would often still be there for breakfast, as there were many rooms for guests to stay, each with their own bathroom and entrances overlooking the sea and the mosque my family attended.

My grandfather was very generous with his property. Travelers passing through or people down on their luck and needing a place to stay were all welcome. More than once my father remembers guests who stayed due to marital problems. Husbands not welcome in their homes for bursts of time would take refuge under our roof. (Stories like this humorously remind me we are all the same, through culture and generation.)

The house faced the sea and was winged with a church on one side and a mosque on the other. My grandfather attended the mosque next door and funded much of its expansion. The church to the south was having financial trouble and was on the path to closure, but my grandfather made substantial contributions to save it. Both the church and the mosque still overlook the sea and peer into the new city of Tel Aviv.

The estate is now a bed and breakfast. I hope strangers are still meeting and conversing on that balcony into the night. I hope little children still try to sneak swims in the fountain. I would like to stay there one day to see if my blood can sense the presence of my father and grandfather and grandmother; to see if I can access their memories and bring life back into the stories they told me when I was a youth. But it feels gut-wrenchingly, soul-scathingly wrong to pay to stay in the home that was taken from us.

ENCHASSI

The name Enchassi means "of Anshas" which is still a city in Egypt. In the mid-1800s this area was still part of the Ottoman Empire. Anshas was the center of learning for many Muslim theologians.

My family can be traced all the way back to the Prophet Muhammad, peace be upon him, through Imam Houssein.

He was the grandson of the prophet who led a revolution against local authorities when he felt his grandfather's religion was being compromised. Imam Houssein and his entire family were butchered. This is why Shia Muslims still remember the 10th of Muharram, the first month of the Muslim calendar, with great grief.

My great-great-great- (however many "greats" span the length of 200 years) grandfather was an imam who migrated from Anshas to Jaffa. In the Ottoman Empire there were no borders. What is now three continents, partitioned up into several countries, was at that time just one expansive territory.

In the 1850s, construction of the Suez Canal began. This canal was important because it was meant to connect the Red Sea and the Mediterranean Sea, thus greatly reducing the distance from the Arabian Sea to Europe. This canal made it possible to get from, say, India to Italy without having to sail all the way around Africa.

Islam, like all other religions, has a spectrum of conservativism. Some people thought the construction of the Suez Canal was evil, as it would change the way of life in the Ottoman Empire—which it did. Many were against its construction because they viewed it as furthering colonialism and opening it up to invaders—which, in some ways, I guess it did.

However, this dangerous feat did not come without a cost. Many oppressed peoples were forced into labor camps to complete the canal's construction. Thousands died of cholera and other work-induced injuries and diseases.

A family story reveals that Grandfather Al-Haddad was a bit of a rabble-rouser and found himself at odds with the authorities in his hometown of Anshas. (An imam is always an agitator.) His exile ran parallel to the building of the Suez Canal, and I would not be surprised if this was the issue he took umbrage with. Whatever the provocative message he preached, it is lost in the silence of history. But it also set him on the road that landed him in Palestine.

A foreigner and a teacher, he became known by the moniker Anchassi. When the British colonized Palestine, our name rolled off their English tongue and came out "Anchasi." And when we escaped to Lebanon, which had been colonized by the French, it became "Enchassi." (The "E" in French makes the English "A" sound.)

NAKBA TO NUPTIALS

My father was 12 years old, the oldest male of six. He remembered it well: the darkness of night, the rumble of the Mediterranean, distant sounds of bullets, fearful murmurs rippling through the streets, household servants whispering through tight throats "Ben-Gurion."

The radio crackled low. Announcers kept saying that David Ben-Gurion was going to stop, but he didn't. His army continued to progress northward. Entire villages were slaughtered. A wave of ruthlessness was engulfing the south and quickly closing in on Jaffa.

My father said the residents took the things they would take if their house was on fire: deeds, passports, a set of clothes, little else. The banks were closed and soon to be insolvent. No money could be collected, no assets liquidated. My grandfather seized all the money that could be found in his house, which amounted to a tin bucket filled with Ottoman gold coins. Thus, my father's family began their exodus to Lebanon.

My father held the hands of his little brothers, with his mother and father each carrying a sister. He spoke of my grandmother in that moment: young and beautiful, looking back at their home with tears streaming down her face, tempting fate to turn her to a pillar of salt. My grandfather assured her and the family, but mostly her, that this would all end soon and they would come back.

"Just a few days," he said confidently, "we will be able to return in just a few days." And like that, the winds of Ben-Gurion blew them to the shores of Beirut, never to return. Overnight, 80 percent of the native population of Palestine was gone—either dead or exiled. Israel commemorates this as a time of independence. Palestinians call it the "Nakba"—the catastrophe.

The money my family had in flight was more than most families had, but only the equivalent of a small vacation. My great-grandmother was Lebanese, so my grandfather had distant relatives who were able to help my family find housing outside of the refugee camp. But the money soon ran out, and they ended up in tents anyway.

My grandfather used the little money they had left to start a small business that could help sustain the family until they were able to return home. He bought a little cart and found some wholesale fruit vendors and became a staple on the streets of Sabra and Shatila, hustling produce to passersby. This way, he would make what money he could, and what he failed to sell, the family could eat and live another day.

My father, being the oldest of the children, carried responsibility in providing for the family. He quit school to sell fruit on the street with my grandfather. My father naturally had light skin like me, but the hours of working outdoors turned his skin very dark, except for his legs, which everyone in the household found amusing. The dark of his face only made his honey-gold eyes brighter.

After a time, my grandfather and father were able to save enough money from selling produce from their cart to rent a small shop within the refugee borders. It was in this shop that my father met my mother. She was temporarily a refugee in Sabra and Shatila and an orphan. She had lost her father at a young age when living in Syria. In Islamic law a child is considered an "orphan" if he or she has lost one parent.

We say orphans have an abundant amount of love within them. They are loved more deeply by their siblings and other family members. At the same time, not having parental love early on, tradition says they develop deeper sensitivities toward others and have an abundance of love within themselves. The Old and New Testaments, as well as the Qur'an, all speak a lot about orphans and how to treat them with special love and care.

> *Righteousness is not that you turn your faces toward the east or the west, but [true] righteousness is [in] one who believes in Allah, the Last Day, the angels, the Book, and the prophets and gives wealth, in spite of love for it, to relatives, orphans, the needy, the traveler, those who ask [for help], and for freeing slaves; [and who] establishes prayer and gives zakah; [those who] fulfill their promise when they promise; and [those who] are patient in poverty and hardship and during battle. Those are the ones who have been true, and it is those who are the righteous.* (Qur'an 2:177)

The Prophet, peace be upon him, was an orphan who had lost both his mother and father. He was adopted by his tribe and had many mentors who helped him become the one who could then turn around and adopt the world. My mother was this deeply loving person that scripture talks about. She was a Syrian refugee, not Palestinian like my father. In the camps there were various factions and, as always, people found ways to make themselves feel superior.

The Syrians said the Palestinians were too dark, that they were savages and violent: If you are Palestinian, you must be in a gang and live in the ghetto. That last part was true, but everyone in Sabra and Shatila lived in the ghetto, so it never made sense to me. The Palestinians were refugees in Lebanon first, and felt they owned the place. In this way they felt superior and had their own slang and racial slurs for the Syrians.

Mutual poverty is not as bonding as one might think. If anything, it reinforces a need to be better than someone else. But regardless of the stereotypes, it is a law of nature that refugees find refugees. In the West, you look for commonalities in personality and hobbies. Refugees fall in love with compatibility in pain: the understanding of your trauma, the intelligence recognizing the subtle ways in which you feel isolated, the fellowship in yearning for a home.

My mother was tall and thin, with light caramel-colored skin and long dark hair flowing all the way down to the back of her knees. She was very modest and a bit shy, but when she looked someone in the eye it was they who became bashful. Her eyes were the most shocking shade of green. She always doted over her younger sisters, praising their beauty, but everyone in the camp knew she was the striking one.

With figs growing in the south, citrus and bananas along the coast, olives in the northern mountains, and fruits and leafy greens of all kinds growing in the Biqa Valley, Lebanon is known throughout the Middle East for its produce. Her first day in the camp, my mother went into my father's shop.

"She smiled at me," my father would say. "I was smiling at all the fruit," my mother would reply. "She kept coming back to the shop to see me," he would say. "I was coming back to see the vegetables," she would respond.

My father became a sleuth in finding out where she was from and where she was staying. It ended up being very convenient that she was staying with his landlord and that his landlord lived directly behind his shop. He would send the very best produce to her every day until he wooed her.

"She ran to me," he would say, "all the way from Syria." Mother never corrected him on that one. Like a bee, she was drawn from her homeland to my father's honeyed eyes.

My parents were always very loving toward one another, though not publicly affectionate. I never saw them hug or kiss, but they always spoke very kindly to one another. My siblings and I never saw them argue or feud either.

Every evening, after a long day of work, my dad would come home and take off his shoes and pants. He'd walk around the house in shorts and a buttoned-up shirt. It was always very humorous to us. He looked funny with his growing belly and skinny white legs dangling below his sun-darkened arms.

My mother was his rock. She took care of all the household, including my six siblings and my father's parents while they were alive. She managed the finances and the cooking and cleaning as well as the child-rearing. My mother was the stricter of the two, but she had the best sense of humor. She was always making us laugh. My father laughed the loudest at her jokes and sly comments.

My parents had a lot in common. My mother had to quit school because her family couldn't afford it. Her father died when she was very young, leaving her mother and her three siblings with little ability to provide for themselves. My mother never learned to read or write. My father never finished the eighth grade.

In their day and situation, education was reserved only for those who had the luxury of having space in their mind to think beyond survival. Education is the gift my parents gave to me and my siblings.

SYRIA

Because my mother is Syrian, we had lots of family in Syria. We would spend our summers in her homeland. My father would take us to my maternal grandmother's house, then leave to go back and work. We were poor, but in Syria, because of the exchange rate, we felt rich.

My grandmother's house was very traditional. Like most homes in Syria, it was made of rock and had a typical Ottoman-style architecture. Her home was meant to be a multi-family dwelling and thus set up more like a cul-de-sac: Imagine a large, open courtyard with a fountain in the middle and lots of potted plants.

The house was built around the courtyard. Surrounding that courtyard were several private rooms, each occupied by a single family. There was one detached bathroom in the courtyard, which we all shared. In the heat of the day the ground would get fire hot and you would see people running barefoot as fast as they could to the latrine.

Every night was like a sleepover. I had several cousins who were the age of myself and my siblings. Sometimes we would fall asleep in the courtyard after spending all day together. All the windows in the house were very deep. They were wide enough that I could sit in them with my back against the frame and my legs stretched out across the width of the aperture.

These windows also served as nice places to nap. On some nights we would pull small mattresses up into the window sills and sleep there as well.

My grandmother's room was in the middle of the crescent-shaped house. It was very small, consisting of little more than a wood-burning stove, used for both cooking and heating the space, and a bed for her to sleep. When we were very young, before we got too big, I remember how we loved to sleep in the bed with my grandmother. She smelled of Aleppo soap, made of olive oil and lye, and of fire from the stove.

We fell asleep with bellies full of her Syrian cookies—butter and sugar cookies small enough to fit in your palm, sometimes flavored with pistachios or other fruits and nuts. I don't know how she could have possibly gotten a wink of sleep with us crowding her in her bed, but she seemed to love it as much as we did.

We felt we belonged in Syria because everyone welcomed us. When we were visiting, the whole family celebrated. Syrian people are very hospitable. It is an important part of their culture. As both guests and family, we experienced the best of it. It seemed we were invited to dinner by a different person every night.

In Middle Eastern culture, there is no such thing as "extended" family. You are just family, and even those who are not your blood relatives consider themselves your "auntie" or "uncle."

During the day, we would sell corn on the streets and pick up whatever summer jobs were available at the time to earn money. Grandmother was very resourceful, as she had been widowed young and never remarried. This left her with three daughters and a son to raise all on her own.

She sold produce on the street just like my dad, and would cook and clean for wealthier neighbors. She would find things to sell and trade and would work whatever jobs were available to make ends meet for her family.

Some summers there were family projects, like a cousin building a house, and we would serve as free labor for these projects. We were always busy, but I have many good and sweet memories of those times.

I have very few memories of ever having fun while growing up. Those I do have are all of times when family came together.

LIFE IN REFUGE

To understand the life of a refugee in Lebanon, you must first understand a bit about Lebanon's governmental structure after the French colonization. Lebanon's politics are under a framework of "confessionalism," which is ultimately a sharing of power distributed among religious majorities. It is a system that feeds on discrimination.

The great post-Israeli-statehood influx of Palestinian refugees into Lebanon was traumatizing to the Lebanese party system. A government with two major factions of power distributed between Christians and Muslims suddenly swallowed half a million displaced Muslims from another country. Christianity was never really the majority.

French colonialism, however, had given the power constitutionally to the Christian Maronite minority. With their constituency shrinking exponentially smaller, it was cause for political unrest, and would eventually lead to a brutal and blood-soaked civil war.

This is why, if you are Muslim, once you are a refugee in Lebanon, you are always a refugee—never a citizen. The government does not want to count you. Even though my father was a child when he fled to Lebanon, he could never become a citizen.

I was born in Lebanon, but I am not a citizen. My children, had they been born in Beirut, would not be citizens. Generation after generation of home-grown refugees is a thick stew for political unrest to brew.

CHILDHOOD

In Lebanon—even though you are little, even though you've known nothing else—you feel your "otherness." You see signs for jobs that say "Lebanese Only." Although there are no chain-link fences or concrete walls dividing the refugee area from the rest of the country, you see the stark contrast between homes on that side and yours. You see the quality of the streets on the other side and the lack of sewage running through them.

You hear your mother say not to go on that side, and strangers yelling for you to "Go back to where you came from!" You are different. You talk different. You look different. You have four miles of "safe zone" in which to travel.

When friends wander outside this invisible belt, sometimes they don't come back. Once my older brother wanted to go with friends to the beach outside of our district. He begged our mother, but she refused to let him go. One of his best friends got picked up by law enforcement at the beach, and no one ever heard from him again. Even in cities of refuge, there are still few safe places for refugees.

It is incredibly disheartening growing up knowing people with their master's and Ph.D. degrees selling wares on the street because your city has no place for them. Educated refugees are just refugees in Lebanon. They are not allowed to even apply for professional jobs.

But my mother didn't care that our butcher was a former dentist or that the man selling bread next to my father's fruit cart was an engineer. We would have an education. She made sure we could read and write, even though she herself could not. She made sure we could speak multiple languages when we finished high school.

My mother kept our hope alive with home remedies of warmed olive oil poured over twisted ankles and ground coffee grains on cuts. Her stories were the kind of magic that healed and opened doors to life outside of Sabra and Shatila.

As kids, we sat and ate and listened to our elders like Native American storytellers. Like my father, they lamented about the old country. We would close our eyes and envision what life would be like had we never left paradise. We imagined having new clothes and full bellies. I thought about what it would be like going to school with my own books and paper and pencils, walking parallel to a clean and salty sea.

We picked up on the accents of the Lebanese people. The Palestinian accent is a much heavier Arabic. It's thick and throaty, made of salt and mineral from the Dead Sea, born in the craters of the Negev.

My childhood developed in tandem with the growth of the Palestinian Liberation Organization (PLO). The elders discussed local politics and the revolution forming. They spoke highly of the nationalistic movement. To them, the PLO was a way to keep a sense of allegiance and ownership over their home country while in another.

In Lebanon, there were many refugee camps, but most of the refugees in Sabra and Shatila were from Jaffa. They blamed not only the Israelis for our plight, but also spoke of the betrayal of our own brethren—the other Arab nations—as a larger cause of our misery.

They spoke of the complicity of Saudi Arabia, Egypt, Syria, and so on, in our execution and evacuation from our own home was a much bigger pill to swallow than any colonial invasion ever could be. There was broad acceptance of the doctrine that anyone who did not accept a Palestinian state was an enemy, that anyone who was the enemy of our enemy was a friend. It was very black and white, and in a way, "cultish," but in the beginning of things we didn't know any better.

We were a tight community. The elders knew each other from Palestine and intermarried. To some of the elders it was important to marry only other Palestinians from the same town. "Her family or his family is from Jaffa," they would say approvingly, even if the actual groom and bride-to-be were both born in Lebanon.

Even though we were all refugees, and our shared suffering should be enough to build comradery among all, there was a lot of infighting within the camps. Each major player in world politics seemed to have a puppet group in Lebanon. There was the Marxist/Lenin-siding club, which of course was a front for Russia. There was a Libyan group, the Syrian sympathizers, and so on, but all united if there was an attack on Palestinians.

The word "martyr" became something we all hoped to be one day. It was so glorified. My friends and I would talk about the day we would become martyrs for this or that cause.

The Russians were a lobbying group among our camp. They paid for influence through weaponry. They took a lot of our neighbors, educating them in anti-American propaganda and training them to fight. All weapons the PLO had were Russian. Any nationalistic conflict happening on the world stage was also fought locally. The Cold War was basically fought on Lebanon's soil.

On top of the devout nationalism dividing us, there was also the ever-present layer of religion. If the socialists weren't being fought for their socialist sympathies alone, they were being fought because "socialists are an enemy of God." Things were ever changing in the camps: buildings getting blown up then shoddily rebuilt, refugees dying and new ones pouring in. We learned at a young age not to take things for granted.

The most constant thing in my limited world was my father's produce shop. Life revolved around it. By American standards, the word "shop" is generous. It was more like a 200-square-foot pocket carved out of a concrete building. Standing in the middle with arms outstretched, my father could nearly touch the walls fingertip to fingertip.

Inside from floor to ceiling we stacked rich mélanges of apples, figs, and bananas in wooden milk crates overflowing into the street. The heart of the shop was not on the inside. The real shop spilled outside in a colorful torrent of grapes, peaches, plums, and peppers.

When it would rain, we would rush to bring in the dry vegetables such as the onions and garlic. The climate is very hot in Beirut and when it would rain, it was like throwing cool water on a grill. The strawberries, peaches, and other fruits would release the most aromatic fragrances into the air and around the market. It is almost believable that my mother really was smiling at the wealthy harvest before her eyes when my father first laid eyes on her.

The shop was little more than a couple of blocks from our house. My father would wake up at two in the morning and go buy his produce from local farmers and wholesale markets. By six it would all be in his shop and ready for sale. We would cause a traffic jam outside our shop during the height of the day. This is because everyone could afford to buy our stock.

My father did not care so much about high profit. He would sell our commodities barely above the wholesale price. He thought we didn't notice, but he would give the very best of his produce to those who couldn't pay. In Arabic, we have a saying, "Put it on my ice tab." Ice, of course, melts.

In the winter we would punch holes in the bottom of a barrel and fill it with anything that would burn—old wooden crates no longer usable for stacking fruit, pieces of blown-up buildings, worn cloth. We would put the barrel in the middle of our shop to keep ourselves, and anyone passing by, warm.

Neighbors would bring more things to keep the fire burning, and it was not unusual for someone to have chestnuts or a potato baking over the open flame. Our shop was truly the community's shop.

By noon most everything would be sold out. If there were still goods to sell, I would relieve my father at noon after school. Many of the other sellers in the market also changed shifts with their children after school. I had classmates running shops of all kinds to the right and the left of me.

After school we would often be hungry, so at lunch time we would get together and share our goods. My friend managing his father's dairy stand, the boy running his family's bread cart, the butcher's son, and I would all meet at one of our shops and together would have a full meal of meat, cheese, bread, and of course, fruit and vegetables. It was hungry work.

In the evening, if I was tired and there was still produce to sell, I would sell it heavily discounted to get rid of it so I could go home—much to the chagrin of my father.

In the summer, when school was out, the produce shop was much more of a family affair. My brothers and I each made carts out of produce crates and mounted metal ball-bearings—given to us by the mechanic next door—on all four sides.

When we pushed the carts down the street, they sounded loudly of metal meeting concrete. Often the wheels would get sandy from pushing them all over the camp. Lubricating them with olive oil when they got too roughed-up kept them going.

We would walk to our customers' homes with a price list of the available fruits and vegetables for the day. We would then load our carts to come back and deliver their orders to their doors—sometimes getting tips! We were the Palestinian "Uber Eats" of the 1970s.

Sometimes, we would ride in and play on our carts for fun. This would often lead to us getting cussed out as the noise they made was quite a nuisance.

Despite all of our hard work, there was still not enough money to be made in the market to survive without assistance. Thankfully, UNRWA (United Nations Relief and Works Agency) provided us with monthly commodities of cheese, margarine, sugar, salt, and canned goods. This was a special program with the sole purpose of helping Palestinians. UNRWA also provided free schooling and clinics.

These weren't the most modern facilities, and they didn't have the most sophisticated equipment, but we could not have been more grateful. Where international aid faltered, Christian charity was there to fill in the gaps. Some of my most precious and formative memories were given by the hand of a beautiful Christian nun named Samira Rahma.

MS. RAHMA

For my mother, as soon as we were born, the clock started ticking on potty training us. Almost by the time we could walk, we were self-sufficient in bodily elimination. She knew that the sooner she could expand our horizons, the freer we could be—even in our circumstances. She knew education was our only way out and our only hope.

The Middle East Council of Churches, which was formed from many different Christian churches in the region, had a preschool a little more than a block from my father's produce shop. It was located in a five-story apartment building, occupying the bottom two floors. The walls were multi-colored, with the Arabic alphabet stenciled across them.

There was a small playground, fenced in by chain-link. It consisted of a couple small benches, a seesaw, and some swings. The seesaw was the most desirable of the playground equipment and was often the source of school-yard skirmishes.

All the children loved to go to school because we knew we would be fed there. Every day when the giant pots of food came in, the smell of lunch would fill the rooms. Having a guaranteed meal was one of the reasons all my friends and I loved going to school. We would try to guess what was in those pots, hoping for a special day in which we would have meat with our meal.

This made learning table manners quite enjoyable. What was not enjoyable, however, was the kitchen lady. She ran a tight canteen. She was a large and villainous woman. She was dark skinned with dark curly hair she wore encased in a hairnet. She was also the school nurse, and she wore the same white jacket when serving food as she did when doing physical exams.

To us, she seemed huge. The pots with lunch were gigantic, and she was able to carry them herself. We would say she ate all the leftover food from lunch. She would check our hair for lice regularly, and seemed to take pleasure in shaving our heads down to a "0" on the clippers.

In the mornings upon arrival she would meet us with a capsule of fish oil. I was only four and didn't know I was supposed to swallow it whole. I am not even sure that I would have known how to swallow a pill whole, even if someone had told me otherwise. My strategy was to bite it and wince the oily mineral down my throat.

I quickly forgot the unpleasantness of this, however, at the initiation of activities with my friends. What was not so quickly forgotten was the disagreeableness of vaccination day.

I could smell it the moment I walked in the building. Everything had been sterilized and reeked of ammonia. The most traumatic part was standing in line. Not only was I going to be subject to gulping down fish oil, but also I was waiting my turn to get pricked. As a preschooler, this was very suspenseful.

These pungent memories are coated with the sweet remembrances of Ms. Rahma. She made every student feel special and important. She would have sweets for us, almonds coated in sugar, and on our birthdays she would bake a cake and bring it to class.

We heard she would walk to class so she could save her taxi allowance to buy us special treats. She would let us sit on her lap, as though she loved us like her own children. All of her students were, of course, refugees and very poor.

Even as a small child you are starkly aware of your poverty. You live on the edge of shame, holding on by the thread in the seam of your jacket, by the stitching in the sole of your ill-fitting shoe. At the slightest pull it can unravel into embarrassment.

Ms. Rahma was keenly sensitive to this state of being in which we resided. I remember her patching up clothing for my classmates, finding extra bits of food for the students who would not have a meal to eat outside of school. She had an intuition about her, knowing what each student was lacking, what each child needed on a deeper level than the physical to feel secure, and she had a knack for finding that exact thing and providing it.

She would console those who lost their fathers or mothers in the infighting. Whether it was

Ms. Rahma with Imad

the hemming of a pair of pants, a bar of soap, or a few minutes of rocking on her lap, she saw our tiny spirits and made them big.

Ms. Rahma was a "consecrated lay person," which is basically a nun who belonged to no religious order. She had taken a vow in front of a bishop to consecrate her life to Christ.

My mother kept us neat and clean. Even though we had very little and my clothes were always handed down from my oldest brother, to my next older brother, and then finally to me, my mother always kept our clothes very clean and was quick to mend any wearing. Because the community shared showers and toilets, we could only bathe weekly, but my mother made sure we kept our faces clean and our hair combed.

Ms. Rahma would bring me to the front of the class and show the kids how tidy I was. She never shamed anyone or pointed out the bad. She only identified the good in each of us and proudly made us examples to each other.

My mother, being the matriarch of nine children (only seven of whom survived), got to know Ms. Rahma well. They seemed to have a deep respect and affinity for one another. Although Ms. Rahma made everyone feel special, I believe she had a special fondness for the Enchassi children.

When I was very young, I caught the measles and missed several days of school. I remember sickly lying in my own sweat when Ms. Rahma showed up at our door. It was very unusual for a teacher to visit a student's home. I had never seen her at our house for my older brothers. I just knew I was in trouble for missing so much school. But to my astonishment she was coming simply to check on me and make sure I was ok.

She had tea with my parents and filled our small home with her big laughter. She showed no fear of my sickness. I felt how I imagined the lepers felt when Jesus visited them, undeterred by their contagion. At the end of her visit she prayed over me and kissed my forehead. This may seem like a small thing, but it changed me.

This was the moment I fell in love with mercy.

GHALIA

Ghalia was my mother's friend and midwife. She was precious to us in the camps. In the camps we could not afford hospitals. Neither I nor any of my siblings were born in a hospital—except for one of my younger sisters, because my mom had complications. I am one of the middle children, old enough to remember the births of three of my sisters.

When my mother went into labor, I was the one sent to get Ghalia. She resided a few blocks away in a one-room flat under some stairs in a building. She lived alone, which could have been dangerous for a woman in the camp. But she seemed unafraid. She was an intimidating human, tall and muscular. She had a voice that when raised would make men put their heads down.

Although she never married, she was asked frequently to counsel couples. Her guidance was often directed toward the men. She scolded them for not adhering to Qur'anic teachings of treating their wives with love, respect, and dignity. Even though she was Christian, they would listen to her. Everyone respected her.

She knew all of our names. She'd be working in the camp and could look at most any child and say, "Your name is _____, and you were born on _____ (date). I know because I delivered you." She kept very detailed and accurate books. Sometimes parents would not register their kids at birth. When it came time to enroll their children in school, this could cause a problem.

Parents would come to Ms. Ghalia. She would look up the names of the parents, then the name of the child and date of their birth. She would then send the parents off with a handwritten note saying she delivered the child.

She was so trusted in the community that these little handwritten notes were accepted with the same authenticity as birth certificates.

She was a one-woman show: a social worker, a therapist, an OB/GYN, a record keeper, a women's health and sex-ed teacher, a women's rights advocate, and much more.

We called her Ghalia, Momma, Mother Mary, Mother Precious. "Momma" is a polite name in Arab culture to call a midwife. She had earned these names in our community. They were how we showed her respect. She was educated and competent, and could have made real money somewhere else, but she chose to stay in the trenches and dedicate her life to us.

I know now that as children we were all very naive to the seriousness of childbirth. When I went to Ms. Ghalia's house, she knew it was time. She would grab her black bag and come with me, bubbling over with decisive frenzy. We knew no fear, only excitement at the arrival of a new sibling. She would go into my mother's room and shut the door. From there it was all in her capable hands.

It was kept very private and was an intimate process between mother and midwife. I only knew the smell of iodine in the room afterwards and briefly saw trash bags with bloody sheets. My father paid her, but I am sure it was mostly symbolic. We would not have had money to pay her what she was worth. "Ghalia" means "precious" in Arabic.

ALI

When I was 10, my cousin, who was a few years older, convinced me to skip school in an attempt to see Muhammad Ali. We were enamored with this big American fighter with the name Muhammad. He was like us, we felt.

Until Muhammad Ali, I didn't know there were Muslims in America. I heard about how he was such a great man that he was able to stand against the most powerful government in the world; how he called his given name, Cassius Clay, his slave name, and made everyone call him Muhammad; how he wouldn't fight in America's war with Vietnam because it was against the teachings of the Qur'an and how he lost one of his fighting titles for it.

My cousin and I didn't know all the specifics or the politics of it, but we were entranced with this hero. He was the first celebrity we knew of to show support for the Palestinian struggle and the first to visit refugees like us. We found out later that the school declared that day a holiday and let all the students out early so they could go meet him.

The traffic getting to him was monstrous. My cousin and I got an early start ahead of our classmates, but we still ended up having to get out of our cab and walk a long way, weaving in and out between pedestrians, to get to him. People lined the street like they were waiting for a parade. It was astounding—all this for one man.

I was small, even for a 10-year-old, so I was able to go between people's legs and squeeze in between people standing shoulder to shoulder. I pushed my way to the front of the makeshift barricades, just as he was about to pass by. He was in conversation with familiar-faced PLO members.

I didn't know who they were, but I had seen them on posters and in newspapers. Every once in a while, he would stop and high-five the kids around him. He stopped and reached out to give me one.

I had to jump to reach his hand. He asked if I knew who he was. I was shocked. All I could draw out of my brain and through my tongue was "Clay."

"No," he said. "I'm Muhammad Ali."

CHAPTER 2

Uncivil War

After my formative pre-K years under Ms. Rahma, I went on to attend the UNRWA (United Nations Relief and Works Agency) elementary school. My early years, though steeped in poverty, were relatively peaceful. In Sabra and Shatila there were always protests by this or that group. We got used to avoiding them like traffic jams on a highway.

The protests sometimes broke out into bloodshed and even morphed into small revolutions, but the violence was relatively contained and we, my family and I, didn't engage. It's not that we didn't care that we couldn't become citizens, or that we were apathetic to the injustices in Beirut. We were too busy trying to survive and to insulate ourselves from the often deadly consequences of revolution.

This all changed when I was 10.

The PLO (Palestine Liberation Organization) originated in 1967, but by 1975, this small Palestinian militia had grown into a full force for the Lebanese government to reckon with. Militia men, with every part of their body covered in black except for a slit around their eyes, would walk around with large automatic weapons. From day one the PLO took on a religious slant. This is because Lebanon was already divided into Christian and Muslim.

In such a place, defining the militia as "Muslim" made it easier to draw sympathies from the already disenfranchised non-refugee Muslims, and it made for good political rhetoric to pit refugee Muslims against Jews. Beirut became a haven for young freedom fighters looking for a cause.

Members of the PLO militia were regarded as heroes. People called them "Fidaee," which is not quite a martyr but along the same lines. It means someone who sacrifices for their country. Although located in Lebanon, our refugee ghetto was no longer under the thumb of Lebanese law enforcement, but that of the PLO. It was like a tree had sprung up through the middle of another tree. We were fighting Israel from Lebanon's borders.

Civil war broke out when a group of Phalangists, a paramilitary group of the Christian political party in Lebanon, attacked a bus and killed 27 passengers in East Beirut—some of whom were Palestinian. This became known as the Bus Massacre. They did this claiming the PLO had attacked a church in the same district earlier. This was the beginning of a brutal civil war. Within the next three days more than 300 people would be slaughtered.

Beirut divided east and west—east being Muslim, west being Christian. Ethnic cleansing was at an all-time high. Both sides committed acts of terror, the most popular of which were car bombings. Every day in our camp we watched for suspicious cars, fearing there would be attacks on civilians by the Christian terrorists. Snipers posted up along invisible lines, dividing Muslims from Christians—two brothers clashing in a deadly rivalry.

Living through this time as a 10-year-old, I struggled to get my education. When you grow up in a war zone, you will come to school and see empty desks with pictures of your classmates sitting on top. This means your friends are casualties of war. (It's funny they call the dead in war "casualties," as though there is something casual about it. It is shocking every time.)

Certain words should not go together. I did not have much education back them, but I knew "civil" and "war" were words that should cancel each other out.

I remember one of those moments from when I was 11 years old. My brother and I came into class to see the picture of our friend, Shadi, who was also 11. He had been playing with an unexploded grenade, and it blew up in his hands. In Sabra and Shatila it was not unusual to see a child playing with shrapnel or weapons. Our toys were the exploded pieces of our lives. A grenade would have been an exciting find for Shadi. I imagine he felt lucky when he found this treasure of war. He would not have known that this weapon was a breath away from detonation.

You come to expect that this war will kill you also. A part of you wants to live. Another part of you wants to die this way as well: a martyr, a hero, a casualty.

When you grow up in a war zone, you know the sound of the sirens that tell you bombs are about to drop. You know to get under your desk and pray: for your mother and little sisters at home, for your father in his produce shop, for your brothers in the building with you and your sisters in the girls' school next door.

I remember going to school and seeing fresh bullet holes in the wall. It is difficult as a child to realize how abnormal and extreme this is. Everyone just attempts to live their day as regular as possible. Teachers continue to teach; students continue to learn. The phrase "elephant in the room" comes to mind. It's like stepping over something large, dead, and tragic in the road and continuing on your way. This is how life in a war zone is.

During the heights of the conflict, school would close for days, sometimes weeks and months at a time. These were the days it was most difficult to pretend life was normal. School added a routine to life that left an unavoidable gap when it was inaccessible. On these days of indiscriminate shooting and violence, everything shut down.

It was like waiting out a dark storm. The family would hunker down in the center of the house so that if an explosion outside or a torrent of bullets rained on any side of the building, we would be the furthest from it possible. On days in which bombs were more of a threat, we and the dozen or so families living in our building would go to a small underground room below our dwelling.

These were the moments where the best and worst of humanity showed up, sitting side-by-side. Outside was the worst: air raids, fires, the sound of gun metal and gnashing of teeth. On the outside were blood and hatred. But inside our small and cramped safe room the beauty of humanity kept us warm and sane. Everyone brought something down into the shelter with them.

Some brought cards to stave off monotony through long bouts. Mothers brought toys to entertain children, and just as in the market when I would take over for my father, each family would bring what they had for their family to eat. If someone only had bread, those with meat and cheese would share. If a mother did not have milk for her child, another who did would provide.

There was no sense of selfishness. No one had plenty, but no one went without. We were the miracle of Jesus and Elijah, multiplying fishes and loaves; watching our meager groceries continue to fill our bellies like the widow's oil filling clay pots.

We could be down there for hours or full days, so we talked. Everyone knew everyone's story—what they were going through, the names of their children, who they had recently lost. I went to so many funerals, I cannot even count them. Many of the dead I did not know firsthand; but in those days, everyone was a brother and a sister.

SHARON

The name Ariel Sharon was infamous among the Palestinian refugee population. Much like the name David Ben-Gurion, Ariel Sharon was despised. He had risen through the ranks as a soldier then an officer. At the time he was the Israeli defense minister, and as such he was responsible for invading Lebanon and isolating Beirut.

There were images of him painted with a devil's tail and horns. Effigies were marched through the streets and lit on fire. He was known to be a fat man, and this trait was mocked mercilessly. It was known that he had suffered some kind of injury and was brandishing a very conspicuous head bandage.

The siege of Lebanon was the impetuous for me volunteering as a White Helmet, a form of unpaid civil defense. When Israel surrounded Beirut, they took over all of the main streets and highways. Civilian vehicles were not allowed to drive on them, or they would get shot at by Israeli forces for fear the vehicle may be a car bomb or means of attack.

We did not even drive the clearly marked ambulances on those streets. We could only travel main roads by foot. And even then, it was very risky. Soldiers would stare at us as we walked by, assessing if we were threats.

The ambulance driver and I were sent to walk the main roads to see if anyone was injured. This was a frequent White Helmet activity. When we would find a wounded person in the streets, I would drag them off the main road and the driver would run back to our headquarters, get the ambulance, and take side streets and alleys back to us.

As we walked the main roads, we made sure we wore our White Helmet uniforms, hoping they would keep us safe from gunfire. On one particular day I saw a small fleet of Israeli tanks, known as Merkava, which translates to "chariot," and a line of soldiers. ("Merkava" is a biblical term used to refer to the vehicle King David rode in. The term motivated the population to engage in patriotic acts of violence.)

Those tanks struck fear in our hearts. It was peculiar to see them out on the main streets unless there was another siege at hand. We had first seen them when they came in to surround the city. When the Merkava came they mercilessly demolished everything in their path. We had witnessed them crush cars in the streets, plow through buildings and people without a single tap of the breaks. It was a monstrous thing to behold firsthand.

However, the soldiers and Merkava did not seem to be preparing for battle. They were protecting someone. Then I saw him: a paunchy man in uniform with a bandage around his head. Ironically, the bandage made him look like an imam. It was Sharon himself.

He was addressing the troops. As I walked by, I could feel hot blood rush through my body. My eyes felt like there was a fire behind them. I stared at him. He must have felt the heat of my gaze because he looked straight at me for a moment. Our eyes connected. I sent him all the hatred and pain I had ever felt.

I channeled all the misery and torment my family had suffered as exiles and tried to burn a hole in him with it. I felt no fear in this moment—only the hot venom of enmity. I believe for a split second he must have felt it. But seeing I was a young boy, he turned his eyes away, dismissing my presence, and proceeded with his pep talk.

Thankfully I did not have an opportunity to act on the evil that permeated my being in that instant, but it was a moment in which I learned that hatred is a very powerful and dangerous thing. It can make you think and do things you would never do otherwise.

WHITE HELMETS

Before the civil war was over, another war broke out in 1982 when Israel invaded Lebanon. A few months before, several of my family members in Syria had fled a massacre in Hama, which had killed many of my relatives on my mom's side. Those members who fled were staying with us in our already cramped home at this time. Everyone in our house fled from Sabra and Shatila to another part of Lebanon, but I, being young and rebellious and full of a naive sense of duty, stayed in the camp as one of the White Helmets. (Our version of "Boy Scouts" actually encouraged us to join.) We were the first line of medical aid and transport during times of crisis. We were basically EMT's, but with very little training.

Imad on the right

When war broke out, we'd have intel letting other White Helmets know where to go and not go to avoid snipers. Sometimes the only way we knew of snipers was after one of our colleagues got shot. We stood at bakeries and ration stations when food supplies ran low to make sure mobs didn't end up killing each other. We ran ambulances and visited those in the hospital who suffered injuries of war.

We even fixed potholes in roads. My friend and I were not even 18 at the time we joined. We wanted to feel like we were contributing to something. Violence was/is not in my nature, but helping the injured and getting them to safety and medical services fit me like the snap of a latex glove.

Israel allied with the Lebanese Maronite Christian Phalangists, a militant group of the Eastern Catholic church and the leading power in Lebanon. Their forces surrounded Beirut. Nothing and no one could come in or go out. It was June, a brutal and airless summer. Not even water could flow in.

Israel and the Phalangists reached up and grabbed currents of electricity before they could reach us, tilled the earth so fruit could not roll from the trees into our camp, dug ditches to swallow food trucks whole, and spilled milk on the ground. It felt as if they had sucked up the wind and suffocated the breeze. Fear gripped us around our throats. There was no resource they could not dam up. It is one thing to fear sudden death, but another to feel death wrap around and squeeze you like a boa constrictor.

A peace treaty was signed in which members of the PLO acquiesced to leave under the protection of the United States Marines. In return, Israel would cease fire and Beirut would go back to its own version of peaceful. I remember this day. Almost every family had members who had joined the PLO. The U.S. Marines came in and escorted them safely to boats, taking them away to Cyprus.

This was a bittersweet day of mourning—relief that the gunfire would stop, but heartbreak that sons and husbands were heading to exile. How many times would we lose our homes?

No sooner had Sabra and Shatila been disarmed when Phalangist forces invaded. We didn't understand or expect this. There were only civilians left in our ghetto. Israel kept its promise and did not invade, but stood back and did nothing to stop the Christian Phalangists. The United States also turned a blind eye to our massacre, washing its hands of culpability.

The first day of the massacre, September 16, 1982, I remember looking up to the hills and on top of buildings, seeing Jewish soldiers looking down on our village in shock. I am sure some of them wanted to help, but were ordered not to.

It is an untrue assumption that emergency medical volunteers are avoided by intentional enemy fire in war. My friend and I hoped, because we wore white helmets and had clear markings on the vehicle that we were not fighters but merely volunteer medical assistance, that we would not be direct targets. But how could we expect soldiers who attacked defenseless civilians to play by rules of conduct?

My friend and I were perfect for the job of White Helmets. We had grown up in Sabra and Shatila. We knew all the back alleys, all the hiding spots and winding roads. A neighbor had donated his Volkswagen to use as a makeshift ambulance. We painted a big red crescent on the hood, indicating we were an emergency vehicle, and placed a gurney in the back along with a very basic first-aid kit. My friend drove and I rode passenger, looking for wounded people in the streets.

They were not hard to find. Many people were sniped by hidden hitmen; others were brutally tortured. People would run at us, wailing that those behind were getting butchered. We saw unimaginable things: missing heads, severed limbs, a pregnant woman with her stomach cut out. We encountered the very depth and breadth of human viciousness, things no one should see. We would take both the living and the dead to be dropped off at the hospital. The hospital was one of the first sites bombed by the Israeli army before the "peace" agreement. What was left of it was extremely overwhelmed.

The first night of the massacre, after having spent the day transporting the wounded and the dead, the driver and I wanted to keep helping. Since we knew the camp so well, we felt we could still aid in finding the injured. We did not make it far before bullets raided our vehicle. I was confused and shocked, sickened because I knew immediately that the shots were meant for us. It was not too dark yet; whoever was shooting at us knew we were medical volunteers.

My friend was shot by the sniper, and the ambulance crashed. Horrified and out of sheer instinct, I opened the door and took off running. As I was running, I passed many bodies, tripping over them, slipping in their blood, until I found a house that was open. Inside there was a small pit with a chimney where the family who lived there would cook meat. I climbed up in the vent.

At this point everything became very fuzzy to me. I heard soldiers come into the house looking for me. I do not know how I pulled myself up into the flue. I do not know how I could have pulled myself up high enough

where they did not see my feet sticking out. I can only explain the unexplainable by giving credit, as my mother did, to God.

I am not sure if I passed out from fear or lack of oxygen—or both—but for the next two days I stayed in the chimney flue, existing somewhere between a dream and awareness. I remember hearing the bullets and the screams. I could hear Jesus' and Mary's name being invoked as the Phalangists slaughtered Palestinians.

I too was invoking the names of Jesus and Mary for protection and mercy. I was in and out of consciousness, until suddenly I heard crying instead of screaming and people howling, "Allahu Akbar," which is a Muslim phrase meaning "God is great." It was then I realized these were my people. So, I came out.

It was like waking up from a nightmare and stepping out into something much worse. It was like the day of judgment. Bodies and body parts were all over the streets. Mothers were crying. I was dazed. I didn't know what day it was. I hadn't eaten. I saw the ambulance we had crashed, but my friend was not in it. A sinking feeling hit in the pit of my stomach. I did not know if he had been alive or dead when I left him there.

I had lost my white helmet, but I was still wearing the uniform. I had soiled it, and it was stained with my friend's blood splatter. I remember desperate mothers coming up to me with pictures, asking me if I had seen their children, hoping that maybe I had been the one to help their son or daughter.

Immediately I started helping to pick up the dead bodies. It was like a horror movie. Some of the bodies were bloated and had been in the street for the full three days. I would reach to pull up a body, and the skin would tear or a hand might come off.

Beirut is right off the Mediterranean. The days were sweltering hot and humid. The air grew thick with flies, mosquitos, and disease. The smell of death filled the streets and our nostrils. We had to drag these bodies—some with trucks, some with wheelbarrows, and some in our arms—while people looked at their faces as we passed by to see if they could recognize any of them.

Mothers continued to come up to me, asking if I had buried their children. It was impossible to know. There were too many bodies to bury, and even if I had buried their child, many of the faces, including mine, were unrecognizable.

Trauma lives in the face. Trauma yoked with starvation turns the face into a shadow of its self. We were all walking distorted shells of our former selves. I wanted to tell them I had buried the child they were looking for, to give them some sense of closure. It was unlikely their son or daughter had survived. Much more likely their child's body was in the pit, never to be identified by anyone.

In Islam, you are to treat dead bodies with the utmost respect and solemnity. But this was a tragic impossibility in this circumstance. There were so many slain bodies, we just had to put them in a mass grave. We would walk up to the edge of the gorge and push the bodies over, letting them tumble to the bottom. White powder, which I later learned was lye, was poured over the bodies to help them decompose quicker so more could be stacked in.

We buried an estimated 1,800 people. I don't remember eating that week, but if I did eat or drink, it would have been whatever the Red Cross or other international aid had brought.

The Phalangist soldiers had taken brushes, dipped them in the blood of their victims, and painted red crosses throughout the camp. I remember most vividly their laughter. It was an astonishing bit of irony that the people bringing aid to our camp also displayed red crosses.

Red crosses were on the ambulances and on the coats of the medics. I again thought of the soldiers invoking the names of Jesus and Mary as they butchered my neighbors in cold blood. But I also thought of how I had heard those names invoked as Ms. Rahma fed and clothed me—the Jesus who compelled her to take care of the orphan and refugee, who urged her to walk to our camp every day and bring us candy. I could not reconcile that Jesus and Mary with the other.

And then . . . I walked. I walked, and I walked, and I walked, trying to find my family.

My family had left the place where they first had gone. I went to the White Helmets headquarters and learned that my friend, the ambulance driver, had survived and was in the hospital. I had the opportunity to apologize to him for leaving. He had no idea what I was talking about. He did not remember anything. He did not even remember that I was there.

He died a week later. He was only 17.

I began my search for my family by going to the area we lived and asking whoever remained if they knew anything that could help me. They told me that Israel would not bomb the purely Christian areas or the mixed ones. Because my family would not be allowed in the Christian precincts, I knew they had to be in one of three mixed areas.

The locality of Al Hamra was the closest, so I began walking in that direction. Al Hamra was where the wealthiest Lebanese families lived. It was like Manhattan's upper east side or L.A.'s Beverly Hills. Before the war, Al Hamra—named after Al Hambra in Spain—was known as Lebanon's most trendy area. Those with resources, of course, had evacuated so many refugees fled there in search of safety.

It was very strange crossing over into the untouched, unviolated, un-Palestinian remainder of Beirut. I could see very clearly that the area I was leaving was semi-deserted but the rest of the city was normal—like nothing had happened. It was like living in black and white then stepping into color.

At the same time, I felt I was abandoning my duty. I kept reminding myself there was nothing I could do. People were buried. I was still covered in blood, sweat, and my own excreta. The area was empty.

Just outside of my camp, the city was bustling with life. I could still hear the occasional bomb detonating in the background. When the sun would set, for entertainment, citizens of this town went onto their roofs to watch the explosions bursting in my camp.

I asked around to other displaced people, inquiring if anyone had heard where the family Enchassi was staying. Someone finally knew of them and said they thought they were in a nearby abandoned complex. I found my aunt. She said my father would have stayed with her, but the building was too full.

She thought she knew where my family had gone. She directed me to an abandoned hotel named Napoli.

In post-apocalyptic fashion, deserted hotels were broken into and occupied by families seeking refuge, including mine. I opened the door to the blackest of black. It was summer, and the sun was high and bright. But when I opened the door of the hotel, the contrast was blinding. There was no running water, and the electricity was off. Once my eyes adjusted, I could tell it had been a very opulent and indulgent place to vacation, but the smell of hot bodies, sickness, and backed-up plumbing diluted its luxe.

I knocked on the doors on every floor, looking for my family. When I got to the 12th and final floor, my heart was pounding with fear that I had hit another deadend. My mother opened the door.

She screamed and slapped me. "I told you not to stay in the camp! I thought you were dead!" Then she hugged me tighter than anyone ever will.

I was still wearing my White Helmet uniform—the same clothing in which I had spent three days in a chimney, the same I had soiled and had moved dead bodies to mass graves in. I was covered in bodily fluids, dirt, and excrement. I know I looked, smelled, and felt unrecognizable. But her arms knew me.

She took my hands and counted my fingers, took off my hat and looked me over. She even took off my shoes and counted my toes. We wept together. We had all seen more than any human ever should.

HATE SPEECH

"Jummah" is a Muslim communal prayer held every Friday around noon. There is a sermon or a "khutbah" given by a male member of the congregation. Everyone joins to pray, then we disperse and go on about our day. Jummah is to Muslims what Sunday services are to Christians.

The Friday after the massacre the mosques were packed. Everyone was looking for answers, seeking hope for missing loved ones, needing to connect with the broader community. There was so much pain and anger—anger at the "Christians" for their crusade-like butchery, anger at the "Jews" for acting as accomplices to the massacre by letting the Phalangists in.

I remember seeing the Israelis shoot some kind of flare guns to assist the Phalangist soldiers in seeing their way into our camp. And there was anger at the United States for assuming a peacekeeping role and brokering the treaty that took away our defenses, then doing nothing to protect our people. The only power many of us felt we had was at the pulpit.

The first Friday after I found my family, we went to Jummah. The khutbah was about the evil we had seen, the evil perpetrated by Christians and Jews. To me it was surreal. It simply didn't feel right to blame the religion of Christianity for this horror. Although I was not a Christian, Ms. Rahma had shown me what it meant to be one. Again, I could not reconcile the two. I felt my belly turn as words of hate were poured on our heads.

One vivid message has stayed with me to this day. It would almost be funny if it wasn't tragically obtuse. The man giving the khutbah held up a box of wafers the local Maronites would take for communion during Easter. He said that when Christians take communion, they say they are eating the body of Jesus and dipping it in his blood. He said in reality they are dipping the wafers in the blood of Muslims, and then he showed the ingredients written on the package: "red dye." He was convinced "dye" was "die" and that this was proof the wafers were dipped in death.

This is obviously absurd and ignorant. But it is not a far stretch to believe such things when you have seen brushes dipped in the blood of your neighbors and used to paint crosses on their homes. For many people, especially those suffering from poverty and focused on mere survival and deprived of an education, hate speech from the pulpit becomes a reality.

It reinforces our most basic fears and preconceived ideas. All one needs to hear is someone in power validate these notions for it to become gospel. Further, when one is insulated from those who differ from them—as in the extreme case of Beirut being sectioned off by religious affiliation, or in the more common occurrence of segregation by class in the United States—a lack of diversity in relationships amplifies hatred.

A specific Qur'anic verse used to villify Christians and Jews is the same one I have heard used to villify Muslims in the West: "Do not take Jews and Christians as [wali] allies" (Qur'an 5:51). Some translations say "friends" rather than "allies." This word wali can be interpreted as friend or ally, but in some cases, it is more accurately translated as "representative."

I had wondered how the Qur'an could say that Jews, Christians, and Muslims could not be allies while in the same chapter it goes on to discuss marriage between Muslims and other people of the book and that they need not convert.

Later, I learned that this verse is often taken out of context. This verse was written during a specific time of war in which a few tribes of Christians and Jews were allies against Muslims in fighting each other. But these were specific tribes during a time in which people identified themselves by their faith more than their politics or place of birth.

The text does not mean that Muslims should not be friends and allies with all Christians and all Jews at all times. It means that a specific tribe of Christians and Jews that a specific group of Muslims were in feud with should not be allies at that time.

The pulpit can be more powerful than the podium of a president. Verses like this can be used to cause massacres. I was too young to speak up, too uneducated. My mother did not buy into the rhetoric. She always knew that people are just people, no matter their race, religion, economic standing, or anything else.

I believe in our hearts we all know this, but some things in this world change us, mislead us, and choke out our conscience. Some of us find ourselves in moments and places in which our moral senses are blinded.

THE HEART OF MOSES' MOTHER

After the massacre there was a rumor that the American embassy was granting visas for those applying from Sabra and Shatila—an unofficial form of reparations, if you will. After the massacre, what hope I had for the future dissipated into the smothering Lebanese sun. I began work as a butcher's assistant to help provide for my family, cutting meats and taking home scraps. I was in a fog.

I no longer felt hunger for food or life. I would occasionally see smatterings of blood left on doorsteps, on concrete walls. I do not know how the earth soaked up so much blood. For thousands of years the ground has been drinking up blood. Will it one day burst with it, like an overripe tomato, blistering and bloated in the sun?

Life in the camp had always felt limited. Now it felt like a prison—overcrowded by both the living and the dead. Even those who lived felt like ghosts. This was not my home. I was born here, but I was not a citizen.

My birthplace would not recognize me. My father's homeland would not recognize me.

At the age of 17 I was finishing high school. I had progressed in my education further than both of my parents, but I had no direction or purpose. I knew I did not want to sell fruit on the streets like my father, and I was not a butcher boy.

My mother, *mashallah*, saw something I did not. "Go apply for a visa to America," she said.

I knew this was a great sacrifice for her. My older brother had already gone to America, and she missed him deeply. It was also a great financial sacrifice for her. For decades she had been tucking away the tips we brought home from deliveries and little bits of money here and there she could scrape away.

What's more, coming back home after war we were poorer now than before it started. Everyone was. This was a not a time when one felt safe to spend savings. But I do not think she thought of that. Through the worst part of the massacre, she knew what it felt like to think I had died—as she was sure I had not survived. Now she just wanted me to live with hope and purpose, even if it meant away from her arms.

The U.S. embassy was on the Mediterranean. Everyone wanted to escape from the wars of Lebanon. You would stand in line all night, and starting early in the morning they would give you a number. You could arrive at 2:00 a.m. and have number 100-something. By 3:00 or 3:30 a.m., they would run out of numbers to give and turn everyone else away.

I applied for every visa available. Each time they told me not to come back because, if they gave me a visa, I wouldn't return to Beirut. And they would stamp my application "Rejected." I was rejected four times.

I went to my father and told him we needed documents from the bank declaring we had assets and a business that would be worth bringing me back for.

The fifth time I overslept. I may have given up and decided not to go had my mother not awakened me and told me to try one more time.

Imad's refugee identification

I had very little faith left. I did not think I would even arrive early enough to get a number.

I walked up to the embassy at 3:30 in the morning. It was the worst storm I had ever seen in Lebanon. The wind was so strong, it was skimming the tops of the sea's waves and splashing them onto the wall we were standing against in line. My hair was soaked with rain and salty with sea water.

It was October 1983, and the weather was very cold. The usher was an American man with sandy blonde hair and blue eyes, who looked at me and said: "You don't give up, do you?"

"I have nothing to lose," I replied. And he gave me the last number for the day.

I shivered in line for hours. When it was finally my turn, I had little hope that this time would be different from the others. The man behind the desk was slender and wore glasses. My entire hope for a future rested on his slight shoulders. He started in with the regular questions.

"Why do you want to go to America?" "Do you have family there?" Et cetera. I was growing tired with the dance and was bone weary from the beating of the storm.

"You live in Sabra?" he asked in Arabic. "Yes," I told him back in Arabic, "but I almost did not live."

I knew he was not going to give me the visa. He got up and went into another room. This is how it always went. He would leave then come back after a few minutes and tell me my application was denied. This time it took him longer to come back. When he returned, he had a visa and my passport in his hand.

I pretended to be sad when I got home. My mother, seeing my face, moved in to embrace me and said: "Oh, don't worry. Don't worry. God has a plan for you." I then broke out in exultation, "I got the visa! I got the visa!" She slapped me again.

Whenever my siblings or I would depart from our mother, she would always say: "*fe aman Allah*" (I deliver you to God). It is a verse from the Qur'an when the mother of Moses sends him in a basket down the Nile.

And We inspired to the mother of Moses, "Suckle him; but when you fear for him, cast him into the river and do not fear and do not grieve. Indeed, we will return him to you and will make him [one] of the messengers." (Qur'an 28:7)

"Maybe the Enchassi name will live on even if it's somewhere else," my mother told me with joy and sorrow in her eyes. For the rest of the day we danced and laughed together, and at night she wept silently to herself.

And the heart of Moses' mother became empty. (Qur'an 28:10)

LADY LIBERTY

We Palestinians have a complicated relationship with the United States. On the one hand, we are angry with the U.S.'s unflagging backing of Israel at our expense. On the other hand, we deeply admire its commitment to freedom and equality.

Growing up in a country where you are estranged from the economy because you are not born to citizens, excluded from power because you do not practice a certain religion, and disenfranchised in every way gives you great admiration for the United States. The idea of being endowed with inalienable rights, and that there could be freedom and justice for all, was impressive to me.

I read everything I could find about America. I read about the opportunities that immigrants have there, about the city I would be living in soon, and about Ellis Island. I began a long-distance affair with Lady Liberty. I was obsessed with her.

She said, "Give me your tired . . ." I was tired. She said, "Give me your poor." I was poor. "Your huddled masses yearning to breathe free . . ." How I longed for it.

"The wretched refuse of your teeming shore . . ." I asked her back, "What is more wretched than a refugee?"

"Send these, the homeless, tempest-tossed to me . . ." I was so homeless, not even the country I was born in would claim me. I had to look up what "tempest-tossed" meant. My English was not so good yet, but this too described me.

I knew Lady Liberty was out of my league—after all, she owned her own island—but she was calling me. It was for me she was lifting her "lamp beside the golden door."

I purchased a one-way ticket to Dallas, Texas, with a layover in New York. On October 23, 1983, the morning of my departure, I heard a thundering sound. My family lived about five minutes from the airport. Something was wrong. I felt it hit my stomach and stick in my brain.

Two suicide bombers had driven into the U.S. Marine headquarters, killing 241 U.S. military, 58 French military, and 6 civilians and injuring an additional 75. This would remain the deadliest terrorist attack on U.S. forces until September 11, 2001, and was the deadliest military loss for the French since the Algerian war. What made this tragedy worse was that the forces targeted were all stationed in Beirut for peacekeeping work.

This terrorist attack notoriously became known in our parts as the "Laughing Death" because the bombers were said to have been laughing as they blew themselves up. Both bombers were Shiia Muslim, and part of the Iranian-backed militia in Lebanon. They were the beginning of the militant movement now known as Hezbollah.

The Marine headquarters was directly adjacent to the airport. The airport shut down so I was unable to fly out that afternoon as planned. I went to the travel agent and scheduled the flight for the next day . . . then the next day . . . then the next.

My passport was dangerously close to expiring and pulling my hopes of a new life in America down with it. In addition to this fear of my documentation expiring, I was also worried if America would even accept me. Finally, four days before my passport lapsed, the airport reopened and I was able to take the first flight out to JFK Airport.

I arrived in New York City in December 1983 with $320. My layover was overnight, so hotel stay for one night was included in my travel accommodations. The hotel informed me there was a tour to the Statue of Liberty for $90. It was almost a third of my money, but I couldn't be this close and not see her.

I had seen pictures of her and was struck by how she resembled a Muslim woman. I would later learn that the original design was done by a French man named Bartholdi who wanted to make a colossal statue for the inauguration of the Suez Canal. She was meant to be an Egyptian peasant woman. They called her "Egypt Carrying the Light to Asia."

But Egypt had already invested more than it intended on the construction of the canal and ultimately rejected the statue. Bartholdi later repurposed his design, and it became Lady Liberty as we know her today.

She too was rejected from Egypt, like my great-grandfather Al-Haddad. And now here I was, his grandson, meeting her in America—as though we had met here for a family reunion.

That night spent in New York City was very quiet. I was used to the sounds of bullets and explosions. The traffic and honking through the streets were too peaceful to me. I could not sleep.

I do not remember all of my feelings that day. But what I remember most was being shocked at how in America I could just take a boat out into the ocean and no one would ask me for my ID or papers. In Lebanon you always have your ID on your person. The necessity of having our papers on us was so ingrained into our minds that we would even take them from room to room with us in our house.

In Beirut, there are checkpoints everywhere. If you got caught without your papers, the police could hold you for days. If they were feeling generous, you may be allowed to go home with a soldier escort and get your papers. Punishment was inconsistent, and there was little due process.

As I looked out at the vastness of the ocean, I felt grief. Knowing that beyond the sight of my eyes I had family I had left on the other side of that great blue, I felt the ocean in my throat and gulped it back down.

The boat was very crowded. I did not expect for the people on the boat to be so friendly and welcoming. Neither the ferry workers nor the passengers were surprised at my skin color or my accent. Everyone looked different than me, but no one looked the same either. Even so, we all had the same look on our faces: one of joy, and upon arrival, a look of deep admiration.

I knew they were feeling the same as I. At that moment I realized I was not the only one harboring a love affair with Liberty. Here were many people she had beckoned to her shores.

She stood towering above us, scraping the sky with her torch, requiring us to look up to her. She was vast and majestic. Dreams so big for me, standing below her, she laughed, and made them feel small and attainable. I was here now. She had called me and was telling me anything is possible.

You had to pay extra to go in, but I had already spent more than I could afford to come this far, so I stayed at the bottom and read the lettering on her base. From left to right, my palms skimmed over the prose in disbelief.

The poetry that called me here from the slums of Lebanon was running across my fingertips. I kept this spontaneous trip from my family for many years. I felt guilty for spending money on it, however not at all regretful.

The trip was short. It felt too short. We deserved a longer stay after all of our history together. But I was honored to have had the privilege of meeting her. The next day I got back on a plane for my final destination of Dallas-Fort Worth.

CHAPTER 3

Lebanon to Lubbock

In Fort Worth, I enrolled in ELS (English Language School) classes. I needed to pass a test to be allowed to enroll in Texas Tech, which was where I planned to get my four-year degree. Until then, I attended my ELS classes and worked a full-time job during the day.

I attended junior college classes at Reese Air Force Base. This was the first time I experienced the not-so-randomness of "random selection." Every time I entered the base I would be selected for inspection. It rarely took much time—just a minor inconvenience. But sometimes, it would be worse. I almost missed one of my classes on one particular day because security made me unlock my car doors and trunk so dogs could go through it all. I am not sure what exactly they were looking for, but I know they often chose to look for it in my things.

After I passed my ELS exam, I moved to Lubbock with my brother to attend junior college at South Plains College. We began attending Friday prayers at the Islamic Center of the South Plains in Lubbock. In Lebanon it was easy to be a Muslim. We didn't even have to think about it. Food was always *halal.* We never missed hearing the call to prayer. Every chore, action, or job flowed freely and flexibly around prayer times.

In Lebanon there is a bit more self-imposed segmentation within the Islamic community. Just as in America, where churches have many denominations and varying beliefs and practices within Christianity, so it is with Islam in Muslim-dominant areas. But in Lubbock, there were too few Muslims to have that kind of segregation. We were all Muslims: Arab, Pakistani, Indian, Palestinian, Syrian, etc.

I started volunteering at the mosque every opportunity I could. In the beginning it was less about spiritual fulfillment for me and more about being in a space with others who looked like me, shared my culture, spoke my language, and knew what it was like to be an immigrant. Even though I came from an overwhelmingly Muslim district of Lebanon, I myself did not realize how diverse our community was. In America any given mosque has about 70 different ethnicities in attendance.

Soon I learned of the interfaith work that was being done in our community and was excited to be a part of it. At the university I became president of the Muslim Student Association and was soon hired by the local mosque to teach Sunday school for the kids and to give the *khutbah*, or the sermon, during Friday prayers once a month. I was the janitor, the preacher, the teacher (even with little Islamic education). Anything and everything the mosque required, I was there to do it.

It was through my teaching Sunday school that I realized the next generation could not read or write the language of their parents or the Qur'an. I felt it was important that Muslims know how to read their holy book in its original language. So I started teaching the basic conversational Arabic I knew in hopes they would develop a love for it and continue to further their learning beyond Sunday school.

Muslims have a very high standard of morality. I wanted the next generation to be able to read our stories and laws for themselves rather than just hearing them from their parents. But every week it was like taking two steps forward and one step back. After a full seven days, my students would forget most of what was taught and need teaching all over again. This work set in to motion the idea of what would later become Mercy Islamic School in Oklahoma City.

As a student in America, for the first time, I learned U.S. history. My professor's name was Dr. Billingsly. He taught me about slavery in America. I thought back to when I met Muhammad Ali and he told me, "Clay is my slave name." At that time, I thought I knew what that meant—or I would have thought I did, had I thought much about it.

This knowledge opened up a whole new brutality to the term. As a child growing up in the Middle East, I had heard stories of American slavery—rumors. Chattel slavery—the American form of slavery in which individuals were in bondage for life, had no freedoms, and were considered property rather than human beings—has no distinct parallel in Islamic history. Although Islamic empires historically often allowed the practice of slavery, as did Christian and other non-Muslim empires, in the Islamic world slaves were treated first and foremost as human beings, allowed degrees of freedom, and were typically provided with avenues out of slavery. Some former slaves, in fact, became great leaders in the Islamic world.

Islam directly ties redemption to setting others free. For example, if one had committed a great sin, one made up for it by setting a number of slaves free. It was a case of incentivizing people to do the right thing. The motivation was redemption, forgiveness, and life everlasting.

I learned of the atrocities committed against the native peoples living in America. I realized that in my childhood games of "Cowboys and Indians," I was playing out the very narrative of my own family's past across oceans. The same story of colonization, the same tale of expulsion from home, the pushing of peoples across man-made lines and territories and the subsequent occupation, the suppression of language and culture: it was not history; it was now. In those childhood games, I had wanted to be the cowboy. I didn't know I was already the Indian.

"America is a work in progress," Dr. Billingsly would tell us. "We do the right thing after we've exhausted all the wrong things."

Still, the façade had dropped. I came to America totally infatuated with Lady Liberty, but now that I was here and we began to have a real relationship, I began to see who she really was. She is not perfect, but she tries to be. She had done atrocious things. But unlike many other nations, she has the ability to self-correct as she goes.

As I mentioned, I was heavily involved in the Muslim Student Association at the college, and it was through this affiliation that I was invited to attend my first interfaith gathering. The Wesley Foundation was hosting an interfaith event and wanted some Muslim representation. They asked my friend and me to speak about the Muslim perspective.

We were both non-native speakers of English and did not yet know what "interfaith" meant. The leader of the Muslim Student Association at that time just told me we were going to do "dawah," which means to do outreach to others. In my mind this meant I was supposed to call people to become Muslim.

It was my first time entering a church. We sat around an oval table. There were only about 15 people present. Everyone, except for the handful of Muslims I was with, was wearing modern western clothing: jeans, button-up shirts, etc. I too was dressed in regular American clothing. Some of those with me wore traditional clothing from where they were from and the identifiably Muslim kufi.

I was the only one able to speak English well enough to be understood. When it was my turn, I gave a long speech about Islam in my broken English and ended with, "We invite you to become Muslim." My friends who came with me praised my efforts, but I knew I had misunderstood something. I did not know at this time that interfaith work is about conversation, not conversion.

No one was impolite, but it was a bit embarrassing—like showing up at a Halloween party and being the only one wearing a costume. However, this was my first interfaith experience and the first time I felt like I had a voice as a Muslim immigrant in America.

NO CATS IN AMERICA

In the 1986 movie, *An American Tale*, Fievel Mousekewitz and his family of mice make a journey to the United States because they have heard there are "no cats in America." Upon arrival they are shocked to learn this rumor of a cat-free America is not true.

I came to America shortly after the Iranian Revolution of 1979, followed by the Iran hostage crisis in which the U.S. embassy in Tehran was overtaken by a group of Iranian college students—holding 52 American diplomats and citizens hostage for 444 days.

Meanwhile, the Iran-Iraq War was raging and the U.S. had sided with Iraq. The Iranian Revolution and the events that followed was the American public's first media exposure to the Middle East and Islam on a large scale and was arguably the beginning of American Islamophobia.

The Islamic Center I worked for became a target for the ignorant. We experienced a brash of hate crimes on the property. Blood was spattered on the walkway leading up to the mosque. A pig was slaughtered and its intestines strung on the lawn. Racial slurs came: "Go home!" "You're not welcome here!" and "sand n_____."

We found slurs about Iranians written on our building and the sidewalk. These uneducated perpetrators did not seem to know that all Muslims are not Iranian, nor are all Iranians Muslim—not that they would have cared. We ended up having to board up the windows for a time because rocks kept getting thrown, breaking them.

Another time a boar head was left on the footsteps leading up to our mosque. I joked that pigs are not Muslim kryptonite. We should start spreading the rumor that we don't believe in eating chocolate or ice cream.

We sometimes had to cancel Sunday school to protect the children from seeing and reading such things. Like Fievel, I was shocked to see this kind of bigotry against Muslims in America.

Finally, we resorted to putting a tall, chain-link fence around the property. It saddened us, not wanting to put up a barrier between the greater Lubbock population and ourselves. But the cost had been many broken windows and hours of cleanup.

"Must we always wrap walls around us, isolating ourselves from one another for protection?" I thought to myself.

Being the president of Texas Tech's Muslim Student Association and an active member of the mosque, I was often called upon to take media interviews. It was mostly newspapers back then. I felt very inadequate doing this, as English was still a struggle for me, but this work felt important.

For the first time in my life, I was talking and making friends with people who were Christian. I found that outside of living in a politically contentious environment in which we were pitted against one another, we could actually have discussions. We could even disagree, but there would be no ill will. There would be no violent outcome. They believed in their faith as deeply as I believed in mine.

In my home country, I would have feared them and they would have feared me. But I found they were kind, like Ms. Rahma.

At this time I had no intention of becoming an imam, but the exposure to working with people of many different faiths through the Wesley Foundation at Texas Tech, and the opportunities to be a voice for my fellow Muslims through my work with the Islamic Center, gave rise to being a part of something greater than myself.

I felt empowered to make a difference in society; to build bridges toward peace. My full-time work, however, was in the food service industry.

RED-HEADED LADY

After graduating with my management degree, I was recruited by Furr's Cafeteria, a family buffet-style restaurant. They sent me to Oklahoma for training and to work as an assistant manager at the Shepherd's Mall location. My first day on the job, an older woman, about my mother's age, with red hair pulled up high on her head and the kind of face that looked like it should have a cigarette in its mouth, looked me up and down and said, "I ask for help and they send me a goddamn camel jockey!"

With a huff, she turned and walked out of the kitchen area.

Part of my education involved human resources, so I knew I could get her in trouble with the company or take legal action and try to get money out of the situation, but I did not want to put up more fences.

Behind the cash register there was a painting depicting a Native American mother holding her Native baby. They were both crowned in a cascade of red hair. It was her son's gift to her, someone told me. She adored that painting. Looking at it reminded me of my mother's care for me. This deflated any comments she punched at me.

I spent long hours each day carrying the burden of every immigrant, seeking to justify my employment and existence through hard work. This was nothing new to me. In Lebanon we did not expect to be given the same kindness and respect as citizens. I set myself to being the most helpful to the red-headed lady.

In Islam it is a tenant to treat women, especially older women, with the utmost respect and care. Also, I did not have my mother with me, so I told myself to give the red-headed lady all the kindness and love I could not give to my mother.

I came in anytime she needed help on my days off, and I watched to anticipate her needs. When I saw her struggling physically, I beseeched her to sit down and I would take on her task as my own.

Every time I would grow discouraged, I would be reminded of a story of the Prophet Muhammad that is found in the Qur'an.

The Prophet once had a neighbor who despised him. This neighbor would leave trash on the Prophet's front porch every day. And every morning, the Prophet Muhammad would wake up to the fresh smell of garbage and patiently pick it up without saying a single unkind word to the neighbor. (If you fight garbage with garbage, it's going to stink.)

One morning the Prophet woke up and there was no trash on his doorstep. He looked across the way and saw his neighbor's camel had not moved either. He knew his neighbor must be sick, so he asked his wife to help him prepare a meal to take over to the cantankerous resident.

He took the meal next door and said, "I realized you did not leave garbage out today; I thought maybe you were ill."

At this time the Angel Gabriel revealed to Muhammad, "Repel hate with love, for when you do so, you will gain a friend out of a perceivable enemy." (Qur'an 41:34)

One evening when I knew the red-headed lady was scheduled to take inventory, I went through all the boxes and organized them, turning them all one way so that she would not have to lift and turn heavy items in order to scan them into the inventory system. The next day she came in and asked, "Who did this? This would have normally taken me three hours at best. Today I got it all done in one."

"I did," I confessed. Her eyes narrowed at me then softened. "Thank you," she said. I think this was the moment we became friends.

She began saving her ire for other poor souls. I, however, became perfect to her—a confidant who could do no wrong. I can't say I deserved this, but I most certainly didn't object to it.

My co-workers called me the "manager's pet," but I would do whatever I could to show her respect and honor. She became a very good and loyal friend to me. She knew I did not have family close and would invite me to her house for dinner on holidays and special occasions.

She spoke of one of her sons passing away, as though it had just happened that day. She was an incredibly hard-working and high-energy manager. She would run circles around any one of us with her work ethic. She was very strict and liked things done a certain way. Even her superiors were scared of her.

Needless to say, the red-headed lady was not much of a people-pleaser. I found myself most useful when interacting with customers, especially when they had a complaint. When she tried to handle them, they often turned into shouting matches. It wasn't long before she was having me take care of any complaints that came up.

Eventually I was promoted and the company wanted to move me to another location. She teared up when she heard the news and called her superiors to fight for me to stay. This she could not make happen, but we stayed close friends even after we no longer worked together.

Being an immigrant, I did not have a clear understanding of what the Thanksgiving holiday was for Americans. Knowing that my wife and I had little family nearby, the red-headed lady invited us to her house for the holiday. This was my first Thanksgiving experience.

It reminded me of the big dinners my mother would make for our large family. The food was completely different, of course, but the feeling was the same. Many gathered around, talking, eating, enjoying the comradery.

Later, when my friend was too weak to work and finally retired, I would often visit her at home. Her home had many pictures of her late husband and son. Her husband was Native American, and her son became a famous artist known for his portrayal of the Chickasaw and Native peoples.

Her house was immaculate. I could see she ran her household as tightly as she had run her restaurant.

She had this huge gray Cadillac that she loved more than most people. It had a leather interior as clean and sharp as its square body. Her son was visiting her one time when I showed up. He took me outside and quietly asked me if I would have a talk with her. The state had pulled her driver's license. Her family had been as nice as they could be while being firm with her, telling her it was no longer safe for her to be behind the wheel.

"She's sneaking out at night and taking that Cadillac on joy rides," he told me. "Can you try to convince her this is a bad idea and that she's going to hurt herself or somebody else?"

I felt uneasy telling the red-headed lady to do or not do anything. "I'll do what I can," I promised.

When he left, and I was alone with her in her living room, it was like she could smell in the air the conversation her son and I had just had. "They're keeping me here," she proclaimed before I could even start the subject. She was not a very open woman with her feelings, but this day she confided in me some of her deepest struggles and insecurities—about age and independence.

She told me how she always felt a need to be in control and how age had taken bits of that from her in small pieces throughout the years. She confessed how difficult it was for her to be confined to the house and to rely on others for small things like groceries and doctors' appointments. She also forcefully and definitively told me she would not be selling her Cadillac—ever!

She was certainly sharp around the edges, but she loved deeply. And she used those sharp edges to protect those she held in her heart.

ROBBERY

Once while working for the red-headed lady, during the slow time of day, I was at the front of the restaurant, giving the cashier a break. A man walked

in with his face covered. "Give me all the money in the register, mother
_____," he said, pulling out a gun.

"Chill out, man; I'll give you the money," I said. "No problem. I'll help
you to your car. We've got no problems here." This is just what I did. I gave
him the money and when he left, I called the police.

Later they brought me in for questioning. After a little while of giving
them the same story over and over again, multiple times answering their
same questions, I asked: "Am I a suspect?"

"Not anymore," the detective responded. "We watched the surveillance
video, and you were too calm. We suspected you may have been involved in
the robbery."

I laughed. "Sir, I grew up in a war zone; I've had a gun pointed in my
face before."

Working at the cafeteria, I was exposed to many minorities. I worked
with and served people of all backgrounds. I learned very quickly to be aware
of cultural differences and to not make assumptions. These police officers
did not understand my culture and the norms I grew up in. Because of this,
they made the assumption that my actions meant something they did not.

I learned this in my personal life as well. In my culture you do not look
your father in the eye for long periods of time. It is an affront to his authority.
When my first son became an adolescent, he would look at me straight in
the face and I would say to him, "Don't look at me like that. What are you
doing?"

But then my wife would tell him, "Look me in the eye when I'm talking
to you." I am sure it was very confusing for him. My wife and I did not even
fully understand each other's cultures.

DREAM FULFILLED

When I moved to Oklahoma City, I had a pregnant wife and toddler in tow.
I had been given an offer by the company to choose between moving to
California or Oklahoma. Because Oklahoma was closer to my wife's family
in Lubbock, we chose to move there. Besides my brother, her family was all
the family I felt I had.

We first met in Texas and attended school together at South Plains
College. She had been raised Baptist, so we got married in a Baptist church
by a Baptist preacher in a town called Loop, right outside of Lubbock. She
and her family did not support my faith as a Muslim. I know that should

have been a red flag, but I was still figuring out what my faith meant to me and how big it was in my life. And, when you are young and brave you think you are bigger than these obstacles people warn you about.

After two and a half years of marriage, I qualified to apply for citizenship. I had shown good moral character while living here, my English was much better, and I had done my very best to integrate into American culture. The interviewers were very kind and encouraging. This was surprising to me, as the process of getting a visa to come to America was much different.

Becoming a U.S. citizen was one of my most meaningful life experiences. Being able to claim a country as one's own and, likewise, having that country claim one back, is something many people have the privilege of taking for granted. On the day I was scheduled to take my oath, swearing allegiance to the United States of America, I sat in a courtroom with dozens of other giddy soon-to-be citizens.

It had the energy similar to a graduation ceremony—everyone having completed their own journey, waiting for their name to be called so they could walk down the aisle of the courthouse and get their own certificate. "This is my rebirth certificate," I thought.

It was a complicated feeling, much like the feeling I had when I arrived in New York for the first time and looked out across the expanse of the ocean. I was excited to be moving forward, but I also felt the weight of what I was leaving behind: How much of my identity am I giving away by gaining this citizenship and pledging this oath? Am I betraying something?

The judge welcomed all of us and named country by country, with each person proudly standing as their country of origin was called. At the end of his list he asked, "Is there any country I did not mention?" He looked directly at me. I raised my hand and said, "Palestine, your honor."

He looked at his list. "The United States does not recognize Palestine as a state. Are you by chance from Lebanon?" "That works too," I said, embarrassed.

Earlier when he had said "Lebanon," another man had stood whom I knew to be a Lebanese man recognized by the government. My traveling papers did not recognize me as from Lebanon. They only identified me as a refugee from Palestine who had been living in Lebanon. This moment was like being introduced to a crowded room by your parents not as their son, but always with the qualifier, "step" son.

I quickly shook off this shame and looked forward with excitement. I was about to become a child of Lady Liberty—a true child, adopted into the family of the free, no longer the embarrassing sore on the mouth the hand covers when smiling.

I was now a citizen of the most powerful nation on earth. This was the family I chose. For the first time I had a document that said I am a citizen of somewhere. And with this, I now had the ability to go almost anywhere in the world. I could visit the old country. I could see my mom again.

After taking the oath, we were all met outside of the courtroom by a group of grinning volunteers who helped register us to vote. I registered Republican. That party's more conservative values appeal to many Muslims, but at this time it had yet to wage war on Islam.

Immediately after registering to vote, I walked across the street from the courthouse to the post office and applied for a passport. I paid the extra amount to get it expedited.

When it came in the mail less than two weeks later, I opened the blue booklet and found my picture inside. I nearly cried. Very few people in America know what a privilege it is to hold a blue passport in your hand. It's a status symbol of your freedom. It's a token of your belonging. It demands you have the right to choose your own destiny and to pursue your personal happiness.

The move to Oklahoma was stressful on mine and my wife's relationship. But overall I was happy. I had graduated from college and had a good job and a family. I was "making it" in America! I was a success by my own standard, and what my parents had barely dreamed to hope for me I had.

However, my happy new world as a young 20-something was soon turned upside down when my wife told me she was leaving. I was devastated.

I was used to having a big family all around me. I grew up in a household of nine people. We were constantly communing with each other, swimming on top of one another like a school of fish. It does lend itself to some discomfort and privacy is hard to find, but there are also many great things about the way I grew up. There was always someone to talk to, someone to understand me or to help me if I needed something. If I was in discord with one sibling, it would draw me closer to another.

When I married, we grew our home from just the two of us to four. Suddenly I was just one again. I had so much fear for the future, fear for my children. What would it be like for them growing up without their father tucking them into bed every night? I worried about their education and their faith.

Having them for the weekends twice a month was what kept me going during this time. I looked forward to seeing them every moment they were not with me. On my weekends I would take them to the mosque. At least I had the freedom to do this at that point. When their mother would come pick them up on Sunday, I would feel her drive away with my whole heart in the back seat.

It was all the more difficult because in Oklahoma I no longer had my brother or my Muslim community for support. It's not that there wasn't a Muslim community in Oklahoma. There was, and is, a thriving population, but I felt I could not plug into it.

In Islam, prayer is an integral part of our faith. We pray five times a day throughout the waxing and waning of the sun. At this time in my life I was trying hard to fit into American culture and to keep peace in my family. I stopped praying all five prayers during the day. I did not hide my faith, but I did not let it "rock the boat."

When I was married, not wanting my wife to be reminded of our differences each time we ate, I would pray silently before meals. I abstained from all outward appearances of Islam. I minimized my faith to something thin and discrete. It was flaky, like dander on my shoulders—something to be dusted off when trying to make a good impression. I learned that when you marry into a family that does not support your faith, you either practice in secret or become nothing. I almost became nothing.

HOME

After receiving my passport, I visited my mom for the first time since moving to America. I was in the middle of a divorce and unsure of the future. Although I carried many losses with me, I was extremely excited to see my mom and share with her my many achievements since moving to America. I had a degree and was finishing my master's and had been accepted into a doctoral program. I was a citizen and had a well-paying job.

It may seem trivial to many Americans, but I owned a car and had a house with central heating and air, running water, 24/7 electricity, and multiple bathrooms. These were things I did not take for granted.

She gave up so much to help me get here. I wanted her to know it was worth it. Having understood what freedom is, having lived and breathed it, it was strange crossing back over into my old life. In Lebanon I am systematically discriminated against, based both on my ethnicity and my religion.

In America I may experience bigotry, but it is not so blatantly government-sanctioned. Despite Lebanon's failings, it is still the home my heart knows best.

As the plane descended, I could tell it had been almost 10 years since I left. The view out the window looked both familiar and foreign to me. The shoreline was as I left it; the landscape had changed, revised and remodeled many times over, through both progress and development as well as war.

I imagine watching Lebanon from above is like watching a microcosm of the history of the world sped up—like those videos of flowers blooming over time, in which a camera records a split-second frame every few hours.

This is Lebanon: war, rebuild, war, rebuild. Such is the fate of every nation; Lebanon just seems to be on an accelerated timeline.

When the plane landed, everyone clapped. It must be a Lebanese thing. On no other flights have I experienced this collective passenger applause, except when landing in Lebanon. We all got up before the seatbelt light above signaled we should. The captain had to ask us all to sit back down while the plane taxied.

Everyone was eager to leave the aircraft, leaning forward, rears more hovering over the seats than sitting on them. Me too: I couldn't wait to see my family. When I exited, I saw my family standing in the same place I had said goodbye to my mom and dad from a decade ago. Only this time, my mom was alone. She was a new widow.

Before they came into focus, I thought I was walking into a demonstration of some sort. But these were all my family members! My mother no longer had my dad, but she was surrounded by an even larger family than I had left. My sister was married and was toting nieces and nephews I had never met. My brother had grown up. I had cousins and aunts and uncles there with more little people I had never met, but only heard stories of.

I had so missed that feeling of being enveloped in family.

Although I had landed, it was still several hours before I could go home. Security had to question me. I had expected this. Any refugee traveling knows this is coming. However, I held my head high and handed them my newly minted blue passport. It labeled my birthplace as Lebanon, so the security officer started speaking to me in Arabic. I spoke back to him in

English, pretending my Arabic was rusty in order to distance myself from refugee status.

Palestinian refugees do not have the best relationship with Lebanese authorities. I knew as soon as he ran my information he would see that, although I was born here, I was not a citizen. He would immediately know my refugee status and Palestinian identity. Any bigotry or bias he had would bubble to the top and make this last leg of my journey as difficult and time-consuming as possible. But maybe if he thought I had been an American citizen for a long time, he would treat me a little better.

After a strip search and hours-long interrogation, I was returned to my patiently waiting family to be taken home. I do not want to speak too harshly of Lebanon. It is the place that welcomed my father and grandfather, giving them a home when they had none. The local people are extremely kind and hospitable.

On the way to my childhood home, we stopped at the cemetery to see my father's grave. He had passed away only a few months before. He was buried on top of his father—two Palestinian hopefuls who never gave up on going back home. They lived and died as refugees.

I prayed the prayer I pray for every refugee: that they will find a home in heaven. I wanted to tell my dad of all my accomplishments. I was a rebellious child, and he did not think I would even finish middle school. Yet, here I was, a soon-to-be doctoral student. I wanted to tell him everything, even my failures.

I wanted to tell him about my marriage, my work, my children, what it's like living in America, what it feels like to be a citizen of somewhere.

I hoped he could hear it all through the whisper of my prayers. My mother was speaking to him as though he were standing there. She was speaking out loud what my mind was thinking.

"You'll be proud of him," she said. "Imad came back. He's a man now. He has a good job. He's a citizen of the U.S."

Returning home, I realized how small the house I grew up in really was. It was huge when I had left it. Now it appeared poorer than before. The furniture looked like the skeleton of what I remembered. Paint was peeling from the walls and the ceilings. But the hospitality was the same.

The whole family came for dinner, and my mom cooked all the things she knew I liked. She made stuffed squash, which I knew took her all day to prepare. The Enchassis are not known to make small meals. She had pounds and pounds of food. Neighbors came by and joined us as well. Conversation around the table was filled with stories of old times and all of our mischief.

Laughter was mixed with tears when we spoke of my father missing from the head of the table. There were awkward moments when the topic of my failed marriage came up, and laughter as my family started plotting on how to find me the right woman.

Jet lag woke me up in the middle of the night. I peeked into my parents' room as I walked past to get to the balcony. I teared up as I saw my father's empty side of the bed. His glasses sat on the bedside table, untouched in the last few months. I wondered when was the last time he touched them. Did he use them to take a last look at my mother's face, or did he completely forget about them in his sickness? How long was it until they began collecting dust?

I looked past his bed to see his clothes still hanging in the closet, ready to be worn. I quietly stepped out onto the balcony and reflected on the change of scenery. I thought of the homes and families that had been destroyed. So much was lost, and yet the same fat pigeons still came to roost on the Enchassi balcony because my mother fed them seed. So much had changed, but so much stayed the same. I felt like a child again in the home and arms of my mother.

The next morning, I went to the massacre site—or tried to would be more accurate. I could not go in, couldn't walk through it. I wouldn't be able to do that for years. Instead, I walked past, along the outskirts. I saw the place where we dug the mass grave. My legs froze. I could see the bodies in my mind. I was there all over again.

I turned my back to them and prayed from a distance for the dead the same prayer I prayed for my father and grandfather: the prayer for the refugee. I prayed they would find refuge in paradise, that they would find solace and a permanent home and be reunited with loved ones in heaven.

The first time back in my father's produce shop made me feel like a kid again. My uncle now minds the shop. I pulled up a chair in the corner where I used to sit when it was my responsibility after school and took in the smells and the energy of the place. I saw old faces of people who used to know my dad.

Word travels fast in Sabra. Many people already knew I was back. Several who my father had given charity to came to me asking for help. They knew

I had been living in the U.S. and thought I must be rich. I gave them what I could, trying to live up to my father's legacy.

Looking across the street to the school where Ms. Rahma taught, I wondered if after 10 years she was still there. I had the urge to get up out of my chair and walk over to see. I wandered through the small yard. Before I got to the inside stairs, I saw her.

She smiled big, and I remembered that smile from years before. She looked so much the same. I had changed, but she still recognized me.

She came over with every bit of warmth and familiarity I had ever known. I told her the same stories I had told my mom and family over dinner the night before. I told her of my successes and failures. She reassured me all things are temporary and that things would bounce back.

As I spoke of my successes, it was almost like she felt they were her successes as well. Her face beamed with pride for my accomplishments. I realized that with every success her students have, with every life lived beyond the confines of Sabra and Shatila, she too is succeeding and escaping.

People say the role of teachers is to teach so their students can surpass them. But now I know that is not true. You never become bigger than your teacher, but your teacher grows bigger with every step you take.

Ms. Rahma reached out and said, "I know I can't hug you anymore" (per Muslim guides of propriety). I gave her a hug as big as her smile.

Behind her shoulder sat her candy bowl. It was showing some wear and tear, but it was the exact bowl she had from when I was a child. It was clear glass with a red cover on top.

As we drank our coffee I asked, "Do you still have sugar candy?" And she did.

New Begin......

I came back home to the closing of my marriage. I lived in a haze. I was back in the chimney, fazing in and out of self-blame and self-assessment. In my devastation, I was at least free to go back to my roots and make connections with my brothers and sisters in faith. I believe that the hard times in life are sometimes an opportunity to come back to faith.

On some level I felt that maybe God sent me this to bring me back to him. I felt guilty about my part in the divorce and like I had "sold out" God in order to keep my marriage going. I buried myself with work and retreated hard back into my faith. When I was married, I had kept the fast but had stopped praying five times a day.

I picked that back up and felt myself getting back to who I was. I plugged myself in to the Oklahoma Muslim community, filling my spirit with things outside of my own loneliness.

It was at this time that the Oklahoma City Muslim Community had split into two mosques. Unfortunately, sometimes refugees bring the politics of their cultures with them when they move.

The country of Pakistan was created to be a haven for Muslims. Many Muslims across India packed up and migrated to Pakistan, hoping to find a place they would fit in. Sadly, they only found more discrimination, as the original inhabitants of Pakistan thought themselves superior to the darker-skinned brothers setting up homestead in the newly-founded Islamic republic.

This political balderdash found its way into Oklahoma City. The mosque split between the original Pakistanis, known as the "Punjabi," and the "Muhajir" (immigrant) people. I, of course, felt most at home worshipping with the underdog. I gave all the time and energy I could to the group that felt exiled from the original mosque. They were refugees, like me, and I felt very deeply, and substantively, their isolation.

In some ways, rejection feels worse when it comes from your own people. I moved through the ranks from member to executive committee, to finance officer, then to president. We were a small but devout and sincere band, holding Friday prayers at War Acres Community Center.

After a period of healing, I realized that I wanted to marry again. I knew this time I would want to be in partnership with someone who shared my values and religion. It was not until my first marriage ended that I recognized how deeply I had been holding my breath. I was heartbroken, but I did not want to go back to breathing shallow again.

They say love comes when we are least expecting it. I was not looking or interested in love when I met Judith. She was a hairdresser at J.C. Penney, and when I saw her smile it was big. The only other person I had seen smile that big was my mother when she looked at my father. I thought she was smiling at me because she liked me. She later told me it was just for tips.

She took a broken heart with two kids and healed me. I must echo what the Prophet once said about his wife: "She believed in me when people doubted me. She accepted me when everyone rejected me. She consoled me when people attacked me. She supported me when people opposed me."

This was my Judith. She was, and is, everything to me.

Judith's family is Hispanic, Native American, and very Catholic. We wanted to get married in a Catholic church, although Judith is Muslim, because we wanted her family to feel comfortable and to be as happy as we were about our union.

Judith had converted to Islam before we married. Her conversion story is hers to tell, and it started before I came into the picture. But suffice to say, if you know Judith, you know that any decision she makes, she makes on her own. And since we married, she makes most of my decisions for me as well.

We had planned to get married at a Catholic church in Oklahoma City. The priest did not mind that I was Muslim, but when he found out I had been married before, he said this was against canon law and he could not officiate. Judith had already invited her family from Mexico, so we did not want to change venues at the last minute.

The priest told us we could use the church, but we would have to find someone else to perform the ceremony. So, we had a Protestant preacher come to officiate a Muslim wedding in a Catholic church. It was a Mexican ceremony, so it was huge.

Judith's family filled the whole sanctuary. I was glad because much of my family could not come. I had 10 family members present; she had about 200. I looked at Judith's face, then out at all the people in the church celebrating with us. This is my family now, I thought to myself. It felt good to have family again.

The Protestant preacher at a Mexican wedding read Muslim vows, which Judith and I wrote on our own. And we started a life that was just that—our own.

Marrying Judith healed me in many ways. One unforeseen way happened much later when I joined a group in advocating for Native American rights at Standing Rock. I felt like this was a way to apologize for always playing the cowboy in "Cowboys and Indians."

THE USUAL SUSPECT

I counted out the money from the deposit the night before; placed it in the plastic bag; and wrote the date, our account number, and signed it. My coworker signed as well to verify its contents. Together we walked to my little brown and economical Toyota pickup. Then I heard one loud thundering rumble.

For a moment I was back in Lebanon, waiting to leave for the airport. Images of the two suicide bombers flashed through my head. I looked at my coworker: she had heard it too. I wasn't hallucinating.

We felt a shock quake through the ground, and she jumped on top of me. She thought it was a gunshot, but I knew better.

JOHN DOE #2 (AKA JOHN "MOE" #2)

On April 19, 1995, the morning of the Oklahoma City Murrah Building bombing, my friend Ibrahim Ahmad had heard his grandfather was sick and was leaving for the airport to visit his family in Jordan. Ibrahim and I were connected on many levels.

He also worked for Furr's Cafeteria. At the time I was a general manager and trainer. Ibrahim had recently been selected to move up in the company, and I was training him for management. We both were married to Hispanic women, and they were friends. Our wives chatted about us in Spanish, and we bantered back and forth about them in Arabic. It was great fun, and we were also neighbors.

During this time in Oklahoma City, the Muslim community had no mosque and had divided into two factions. The one both I and Ibrahim belonged to met in an apartment every week for worship. I was a leader for this group and sometimes gave Jummah, or the sermon, before prayers on Friday afternoons.

Ibrahim knew he was about to get his own location to manage and knew if he was going to travel, he needed to do it sooner rather than later. He also had word that his grandfather was not doing well, and he wanted to see him one last time. The plan was for him to visit his family in Jordan while his wife traveled to visit her family in Mexico.

Ibrahim's family in Jordan, especially his younger nieces and nephews, were very interested in American electronics. So prior to leaving, he went to Radio Shack and purchased an array of small and affordable electronics as gifts for his family abroad.

Ibrahim's flight was scheduled on the morning of April 19. As customary for many Muslims, Ibrahim was running late that morning. His friend pulled up to his home to pick him up and take him to the airport. His neighbor looked out the window to see two Muslim men rushing to throw duffle bags in a vehicle then speed off.

After news of the Murrah Building bombing, this neighbor promptly called the FBI to report the suspicious behavior of these dubious individuals—giving a description of two brown men with large noses, beards, and curly hair. Ibrahim was stopped at his layover in Chicago and questioned for roughly three hours by airport security, then another three hours by the FBI.

They started out by asking general questions: "How long have you been here? When did you become a citizen?" Then they started asking questions regarding the Muslim community at large: "Do you know how many Muslims are in Oklahoma City? Do you pray? Do you go to the mosque?"

Ibrahim answered all their questions, confirming he was a devout Muslim, that he did pray and fast and go to mosque. Eventually the FBI let him go and allowed him to resume his journey.

By then, he had missed his connecting flight and was redirected to Heathrow Airport in London where he was detained again and questioned. This time, they stripped him naked and did a search. This is an extremely humiliating invasion of privacy for anyone, but for a Muslim in particular it is humiliating. We are a very modest people.

During their search, security found the cluster of electronics in his luggage that he had purchased as gifts, which they deemed potential "bomb-making materials."

Security handcuffed Ibrahim and put him on a plane back to the States, sending him to Washington D.C. By this time, the media had been told that a man of Middle Eastern descent had been detained and was being picked up in D.C. Upon arrival, he was taken to a van and read his Miranda Rights.

News of Ibrahim's detainment quickly reached the U.S. Soon his photo was plastered all over the media, identifying him as John Doe #1. The media reported his wife had fled to Mexico, insinuating she had known of the bombing in advance. In truth, she was scheduled to leave for Mexico the next day but had not yet left.

I remember that night seeing footage of his house on the news. There were images of his wife outside the door in her hijab. She was trying to hide her face from the media with a packet of Pampers diapers. I stood there dumbfounded, thinking, "How could this be? This is not right."

Once word of Ibrahim's address got out, he and his wife received death threats and their home was vandalized by people dumping trash on their lawn and worse. My wife and I knew it was not safe for Ibrahim's wife to remain in her home, so we brought her to ours.

At this point the media had been so convincing that even I was skeptical of my own friend's innocence. I attempted to go into work the next day, but I could not make it through. The hate was palpable in my restaurant.

An older gentleman who had been coming in for years, and with whom I thought I had a good relationship since he had even been to my home for dinner once, turned against me. "You people better not have done this!" he yelled with a pointed finger at me as he left from eating his lunch.

With the publication of Ibrahim's photo, the news also released a sketch of John Doe #2, based on the description the neighbor had given. It looked like any Muslim man. The media focused on our community of worship, calling us the "seceding group" since we met at an apartment weekly—insinuating we were some kind of sleeper cell.

They also fixated on this man's occupation at Furr's, spotlighting coworkers as potential accomplices to the terror attack. I knew it was only a matter of time before I was identified as John Doe #2.

Even the vehicle description the neighbor had given, a brown truck, fit my vehicle. I turned myself into FBI headquarters. I did not know if Ibrahim was innocent or not. In all honesty, I had succumbed to the power of the media's message, and thought maybe Ibrahim had done this horrible thing. I just wanted to clear my name and do my best to prove I had nothing to do with any of it.

To my surprise, I was brushed aside completely. I was told to go home, and if further information was needed they would let me know. The other Muslim men who suspected they, too, were John Doe #2 were also dismissed. About a day and a half later, Timothy McVeigh was identified as the terrorist.

It is my theory that the FBI knew the Muslim community was not at fault the whole time and used us as a decoy. The bombing happened on the two-year anniversary of the Waco siege in which U.S. federal forces along with Texas state law enforcement carried out a botched raid, leading to the deaths of 76 civilians. The Murrah Building housed several federal agencies that had played a part in the Waco siege.

Several Oklahoma Muslim families were devastated during this time by the unrelenting media coverage of our community. Even after Timothy McVeigh and Terry Nichols were identified, the news did not stop profiling us. Some outlets were convinced that McVeigh and Nichols had connections to the Middle East somehow.

Rumors spread that Nichols had an insidious acquaintance in Indonesia and that McVeigh knew a contact in some other predominantly Muslim country. I cannot recall all the incredible and bizarre rumors. So-called "Muslim experts," such as Steven Emerson, said things like, "This has Middle Eastern prints all over it."

What makes someone a "Muslim expert"? Do they eat tabbouleh for breakfast and hummus for lunch? Do they sleep on pillows made of falafel and substitute strong coffee for alcoholic beverages?

I remember one man, in particular, who was harmed by the media frenzy. He was a political refugee from Iraq living in America. He, like myself, had seen many horrors. He struggled deeply with his mental health.

His name was Hussein Hussein. The media started following him, convinced he was connected somehow to Timothy McVeigh. Hussein thought it was the Iraqi government coming after him. He was paranoid that the dictator of Iraq, Saddam Hussein, had sent assassins to kill him.

This speculative and completely unnecessary invasion of his privacy by the media completely broke his mental health. He ended up homeless and lost his family. He came to me for advice once. I tried to pull reality down within his grasp and attempted to get him professional help, but I was ultimately unsuccessful. I think of him often, wondering if there is something else I could have done.

The Muslim community never received any kind of apology for our targeting. The world just moved on. They kicked us and left us with dirt in our mouths. But it is in times of hardship and crisis that love and friendship shine the brightest.

The Oklahoma Interfaith Alliance was established immediately, and because of this incident Oklahoma has one of the strongest interfaith communities in the country. The Murrah Building bombing was the first time we were put to the test, and I believe it is the reason we as a state are so good at interfaith work. We have had more time to practice.

During this time, many Muslim women in Oklahoma were fearful for their safety because their headscarf, or hijab, made them easy targets for hate. In response, several Christian congregations volunteered their church vans to transport these women to their places of worship.

The Council on American Islamic Relations (CAIR) came in from Washington D.C., to help the Oklahoma Muslim community during this difficult time. We didn't know how to do anything pertaining to public relations. CAIR helped us draft press releases and coordinate conferences. They also assisted in legal representation for those who needed it. We all wanted to move toward healing.

The very first donation made to the Murrah Building Memorial was a $5,000 check from the Muslim community. Once Ibrahim was exonerated and back home in the States, he wanted to make sure his neighbor who reported him knew there were no hard feelings. So, we decided to bake her a pie and take it over to her house. She apologized profusely, and Ibrahim told her he forgave her and that he understood she was only trying to carry out her civic duty.

9/11

Judith and I had just built our first home. For an immigrant, and especially for a refugee, home ownership is the ultimate dream. It's the standard by which you measure if you've escaped or not. My modest home in America was 10 times that of my childhood home in the camp.

It had central heating and air, something that no matter how long I live in America I will ever take for granted. I remember very vividly the new carpet and the smell of fresh paint, deciding where to situate the furniture and bare mattresses laid up against the wall as we put together the bed frame.

Our few pieces of furniture struggled to fill up the house, but we occupied it with hope. We looked forward to a happy life in our new home and with a large family.

We moved in over Labor Day. I was in charge of unpacking the electronics. The gas had not been turned on yet. We were still taking cold showers, patiently waiting for "sometime between 8:00 a.m. and 7:00 p.m." the next Tuesday, when the service was scheduled to come out.

We were also waiting for our cable TV to be set up. Because we did not have local channels yet, I hooked up to satellite and turned on the Dubai news station on silent as I moved boxes in and out of our new house. I was lucky enough to have friends helping me bring in large items.

I kept seeing on the TV a looping image of a plane crashing in to a tall building. I recognized it as the Twin Towers from my trip through New York City. I thought it was a plot device from a science fiction movie I hadn't seen yet, or perhaps a contrived news segment scene used to push the narrative along.

Then my phone started ringing. I turned on the TV's sound. All of us sat down on the floor, mesmerized and in complete shock at the images on the screen.

I started taking the calls coming in. They were all saying the same things: "They think the hijackers were Muslim . . . How could anyone do this in the name of Islam? . . . I don't know if we will be going to Jummah prayer this Friday."

We hadn't forgotten the scrutiny and distrust that arose from the Oklahoma City Murrah Building bombing. Our community was bracing itself for backlash and biting our metaphorical nails for fear of misplaced retaliation.

Our masjid, or mosque, had opened in December 1997, so at this point it was only a few years old. The FBI began knocking on doors and questioning members of the congregation. Two agents came in to my restaurant and flashed their badges to a waitress who was an immigrant from Russia. She met me in the back to inform me of their presence.

"The FBI is out front looking for you," she said to me with a straight face and the jumpiness you see in a wild animal's eyes. "Do you want to leave now out the back door?"

I went to the front to greet the agents. "It's not a good tactic to flash your badges at people," I said. "It makes them nervous and gives them the reputation of being in trouble for something."

As the agents ate fried chicken thighs and potato salad, they asked me about a man named Moussaoui who had attended our mosque. "I do not believe I know this person," I said.

I remembered hearing that when speaking to law enforcement, one should always request legal counsel. The exchange became very short after that. The agents left, and I finished up my workday after calling Judith to let her know what had happened.

Our community was awash with fear. We remembered all too acutely the devastation from the Murrah Building bombing. We remembered mourning as Oklahomans and simultaneously mourning the harassment we were subjected to, wrought through false allegations and bigotry.

What would it be like this time, now that the men who had done this atrocity were identified as Muslim? How bad would it get now that those who hated our community felt justified?

The media poured into the mosque for a reflection shortly after the attack. At the time, our imam was Suhaib Webb, a Muslim convert from Christianity. I could tell the media was disappointed the imam was a white guy.

After the 1995 Murrah Building bombing, we learned that we must get ahead of hate as best we could. In Islam, it is better to give humbly in secret, but we now know that when our community is the target, we need to do our good deeds in a more public manner.

Our mosque donated to the widows' fund for the loved ones left behind after 9/11. Governor Frank Keating came to Mercy School and publicly accepted the check as the children recited the Pledge of Allegiance. Then the children walked across the street to the mosque, bringing their American flag with them.

A picture appeared in Oklahoma's most widely distributed paper, *The Oklahoman*, of the children reciting the pledge in the mosque while looking at the flag. This did not go over well with some of our community members. Islam is strictly monotheistic. Our religion discourages the use of idols. As the term "idol" is somewhat vague, there are varying views on what is considered an idol and what should and should not be in a mosque.

Some Muslims are against all imagery and symbols being present in our house of worship. They felt we were kneeling to fear and giving up some of our principles. However, this is not merely an Islamic issue. Churches have had the same contentions over having flags in their halls, although present-day debates over the need for an American flag in a house of worship seem to hinge more on the folly of equating patriotism with godliness.

In Oklahoma, I felt the unspoken apology for the Murrah Building bombing came after 9/11. The Oklahoma media seemed to take on a cautious reticence they lacked following the OKC bombing. The aftermath of 9/11 for the Oklahoma Muslim community was quiet compared to that of the Murrah bombing. There were only a few hate crimes Oklahoma Muslims experienced in direct response to 9/11.

I remember a Muslim boy in Broken Arrow getting beaten up and a Muslim-owned pizza shop getting a brick thrown through the window, but these were easier pills to swallow compared to our past experience. The most difficult part was dealing with the sheer panic we felt in our bellies. Men shaved their beards. Those wearing robes traded them in for a suit and tie— looking more like Baptists wearing a funny hat.

Many women who wore hijabs started wearing wigs to cover their heads or just stopped going out altogether. At the Friday prayer after 9/11 our masjid was only half full. The fear in our community was an ear-piercing dog whistle only we could hear.

Our greatest blessing was the outreach of the interfaith community. Rabbi Packman from the Oklahoma City Reform Synagogue offered support and expertise since the Jewish community was no stranger to persecution. We had Christian preachers calling to ask if we needed security.

Neighbors brought flowers to our mosque in an overwhelming show of solidarity. They were piercings of light through the dark cloud that hung over us.

The FBI continued to question me about Moussaoui, who was officially identified as the "20th hijacker." He became known for saying, prior to 9/11, that he wanted to learn how to fly a plane but didn't want to learn how to land.

I did not remember ever meeting Moussaoui and knew I had not spoken to him on the phone. But according to his phone records, he had placed two calls to me, both exactly 30 seconds long. This meant his calls went to my voicemail.

I learned later that Moussaoui had contacted me, trying to find a wife. I was the unofficial matchmaker of Oklahoma City. I was famous for knowing everyone and was pretty good at putting two people whose personalities I thought would complement each other in a room together and letting it go from there. Although I never matched Moussaoui with a wife, Moussaoui matched me on multiple dates with the FBI!

I watched imams, often from other countries, whose first language was not English, struggle to communicate the feelings of our community. It was what I had experienced in Texas when vandalism and hate crimes occurred. This time, I had a much better grasp of the English language and had experience working with the interfaith community.

Islam is shared by a great swath of people, spanning many diverse cultures. I could see in the wake of the 9/11 tragedy that we needed to be more united as a religion. It was important to put aside our own differences as Pakistani Muslims and Saudi Muslims, Indian, Palestinian, etc. We needed to develop an identity as American Muslims. In my khutbahs I began to preach about what united us as Muslims in America.

"What does the money in your pocket say on it?" I would ask. "It says United States of America. Where are your children born and your grandchildren? And more importantly, what language am I giving khutbah in? There are 72 different ethnicities represented here in this mosque, and this language—English—binds us together. This and Arabic—the language in which our holy book was written—unite us today as American Muslims. Here, there is not a distinction between Arab and Pakistani, Sunni or Shia; we are all Muslim."

We raised the American flag on the mosque property in direct response to 9/11. This was for both our community and for those not practicing Islam. It was a statement to Oklahoma Muslims that we are all Americans. We do not live in isolation. We want people to be proud of their heritage, but to pay attention to their future here.

I didn't want them to make the same mistake as my grandfather who was always looking back toward home, never truly living again in his displacement. Only when you feel you have an identity and think of this place as your country can you establish yourself and excel within a society. It was also a message to those of other faiths, that we are just as much American as they are.

I felt I had a perspective that could reach across borders. I grew up Muslim in the East, and having only been 17 when I arrived on the shores of America, I felt I had done a lot of growing up in the West as well. I could relate to both cultures. I could eat pumpkin pie topped with hummus!

I began to think about becoming an imam, but I was not the first to consider that possibility.

IMAD

Pregnant with me and uncomfortable in the hot sun, shielding her eyes from the reflection of the heat and light off the never-ending concrete of Sabra and Shatila, my mother walked home from my father's produce shop. An imam she had never met before stopped her in the street and said, "You will have a boy. You must name him Imad Uddin, for he will be an imam and a pillar of the faith. (Imad means pillar.) He will unite many feuding people."

My mother was not religious in her younger years. At this time, she was not even *hijabi*, meaning she didn't cover her hair by wearing a hijab. For both my parents, until they were much older, Islam was mostly cultural, not much of a personal or spiritual walk. Even so, it is not unusual in Islamic culture to seek the advice of an imam when naming a child.

She originally wanted to name me "Basam," which means "always smiling" in Arabic, but having been given a word from a mysterious imam, she told my father my name should be "Imad Uddin." "It's too long" he said. So, they shortened it and just named me "Imad."

I feel this shortened name is much more fitting for me anyway. Just as the longer version would feel a bit grandiose, so do I feel is this story. I struggled whether or not to even tell it, not wanting anyone to think I am prideful or that I see myself as special among others. I do, however, feel as others that I have a purpose in life.

It was not until after I became an imam and started my interfaith work that my mother mentioned this story to me. Funny how she just watched prophecy unfold quietly. Perhaps she felt she should not interfere with Allah's plans, or perhaps she simply forgot the prediction until she saw it fulfilled.

When I graduated from high school, I told my father I wanted to go to school to become an imam. He told me imams don't make enough money and that imams get assassinated. In Lebanon, because the government is tightly woven with religion, an imam is not just a religious position; it is also political.

CROSSING BORDERS AND BOUNDARIES

Just as many Americans felt the urge to join the military after 9/11, I felt a calling inside of me to become an imam and spread peace and understanding. But I knew I wanted to learn the Qur'an and Islam from the source.

I didn't want to learn from the English translation or from the Western perspective. I had heard through the grapevine that an imam who had taught me as a child had opened a school in Lebanon. I applied to his school for an eight-year program.

For the next eight years I spent four months at a time during the summer in Lebanon and one month every winter. During these bouts of time in Lebanon, I would work one-on-one with my professor and test with the other students.

When I came home, I brought my curriculum with me and studied with a local imam and professor at Oklahoma University. It was interesting and valuable learning from a Western perspective and then relearning from an Eastern one.

When I went back overseas, my brain was constantly comparing the two and thinking about what interpretations make the most sense for the world I live in and how to explain these concepts to an audience in Oklahoma.

An example of this is that, under classical Islamic law, when a couple is married, the woman must have a representative negotiate the marriage contract for her regarding her dowry, or spousal gift. Classical Islam thought it would be more appropriate for a man to negotiate with another man. This is often a father, a brother, or an uncle—anyone who would have her best interests in mind.

Further, this representative should be of the same faith as the bride so as not to create an alliance and to negotiate in a way more favorable to the groom rather than the bride. An example would be if, say the bride was Christian and the groom Muslim, Islamic law would say the bride's representative must also be Christian. Because if this representative were Muslim, like the groom, he may negotiate in a way that is more favorable to the groom simply because they share the same faith.

There are four classical imams that ruled on this issue. Three insisted on the bride needing a representative. One concluded there is enough evidence that a woman can speak for herself. Obviously, this last ruling is more appropriate in the West. So, this is the ruling that guides the way in which I perform weddings.

However, in societies that are still highly patriarchal, the system of requiring a fair advocate for the woman seems to be making an unjust system as just as it can be. We have to remember that through time and across different cultures, norms change and we cannot judge another culture by our own standards. We all have blind spots, and something that looks archaic to us may have been a step toward equality and highly progressive in another time.

Although I was exhausted for eight years traveling back and forth, it was the only way I could receive a traditional Islamic education overseas while continuing to establish my life in the U.S. It was also a chance to spend time with my mother, who still lives in the tiny home in which I grew up in the camps of Sabra and Shatila.

Although I had achieved both my undergrad and graduate degrees in business management and human resources, I had to start back at a high school level. I had to relearn my language of Arabic. I thought I knew my own language, but classical Arabic is extremely difficult.

My second summer in, I almost gave up. It was sweltering in Lebanon, and I had to wear a miserably hot and long robe along with a hat as a uniform.

In frustration and defeat, I took off my hat and cloak and told my brother over the phone, "This is not for me. I can't do this. I'm too far behind."

I laid down for a nap and woke up to the imam I had trained under as a child rubbing my feet. I sat up quickly and pulled my feet away. "I heard you are quitting," he said to me.

"Yes," I said. "I am too far behind. I can't keep up."

"I will not only rub your feet, I will kiss your feet," he said. "We need you to portray the real, loving Islam in the West."

He told me to be at his home at 3 o'clock every morning and he would tutor me in classical Arabic. So, I did. For years I studied under him. I owe to him all the knowledge I have. He too believed in interfaith work, although for him, in Lebanon, it was not only reaching out to different religions but also reaching out to different sects of Islam.

During my studies, I kept my American citizenship under wraps. I hid it for a few reasons: I didn't want anyone censoring themselves around me or thinking of me as an outsider. I was already much older than many of the other students, and I had a bit of an accent when speaking Arabic. My Arabic professor told me I spoke Arabic with an "Okie accent." My perspective was also different than many. My professors knew, however, that I had been living in America. They were not surprised by my sometimes Western-tinted outlook when studying the holy scripture.

One professor told me that was the beauty of Islam. It was written to transcend human constructs and could be applied contextually in any culture.

I also hid my citizenship out of fear. I knew from growing up in Lebanon that some might see my American citizenship as a betrayal to Palestine and the PLO movement. There is also a lot of anti-American sentiment there. On more than one occasion, I was asked to take a selfie or a picture with someone when visiting their home, and there would be anti-American propaganda on a poster or something in the background I would not want to be seen with.

Even though I looked like the other students and spoke Arabic, my teacher warned me to keep my citizenship a secret. His warnings for caution were well founded. At one point a student who had suspicions about me searched my name online and found out I lived in the States. He started spreading rumors that I was a spy and trying to infiltrate the seminary.

My teacher held a seminar for all 600 students, telling them I had grown up with them in Sabra and Shatila, that I had lived through the massacre and helped take care of the wounded and bury the dead as a White Helmet. He then told them I was now an imam in the West. After this information was revealed, the rumors stopped and fellow students started asking me to help them with their English, and asked me questions on how to get to America and if I could help with that too.

This is the irony of our nation. Somehow it is both loved for its freedom and detested for its foreign policy.

American imams get it from both sides. In America they are often targeted by hate speech from politicians and harassed by the FBI. In the Middle East they are at risk of being kidnapped and made an example of by terrorist organizations. Western imams also find themselves on hitlists for speaking out against Al-Qaeda and ISIS.

The day Osama Bin Laden was captured, I made a statement to the media about his death that it was a relief this chapter finally felt like it was coming to a close. I received two calls almost immediately from an overseas blocked number. The voice left a message saying, "You too will have a burial at sea for what you said about Bin Laden."

This is the event I told the FBI and no one else about because I did not want my wife to worry. Later, when I would travel to Palestine, Israeli intelligence would bring this up in my interrogation.

Another time I stood in Oklahoma City's Penn Square Mall with some of my fellow Muslim brothers and sisters with signs reading, "ISIS does not represent me." Because of this, ISIS put me on their "secondary" hitlist. The media asked me what I thought of that, and I said it was a badge of honor to be on an ISIS hitlist.

In those eight years of back-and-forth travel and study, I received a bachelor's degree in Islamic Studies, a master's in Islamic Leadership, and a Ph.D. in *Dawa* (outreach). My Ph.D. thesis concentrated on the constructive effects of 9/11 on the Muslim community. Emphasis was on the word "constructive," which does not mean "positive."

As evil and wicked as 9/11 was, it had constructive effects on the Muslim community. I spoke of the techniques employed by Muslims in the West to promulgate their faith in a positive way—highlighting how Islam was portrayed in the West by the media.

It changed individuals and families and whole communities. Individuals became more integrated into their local communities—participating in neighborhood watches, joining school boards, and engaging in interfaith work. We started becoming more integrated into the system. It was like we were forced to go from being adolescents to adults overnight.

We started taking more ownership in our country. We started opening food pantries, nonprofits, and clinics. Our view of our own social relevance changed. We took our heads out of the sand and started participating civically and standing up for the civil liberties of ourselves and others. There was an emergence of young Muslim artists.

We are typically encouraged to pursue degrees in medicine and engineering. You can look at charts and see how after 9/11 there was a shift in studies among Muslim students, many switching their college majors to the pursuit of art. There were case studies of students in their second or third year of medical school taking a 180-degree turn and finishing their degree in literature or something else related to the liberal arts.

We had comedians, authors, poets, journalists (my own daughter became one), and performers of all kinds who wanted to portray their real faith in Islam. Art, I argued in my thesis, is the outward cry of an inward hurt. My thesis was that this was, at least in part, a response to the atrocities of 9/11.

When defending my thesis, I recounted a joke by a Muslim comedian: "I'm not responsible for 9/11 . . . maybe 7-11." Nobody laughed. One of them asked, "What happened July 11? Did America accuse us of July 11?" I had forgotten they don't have 7-Eleven convenience stores in Lebanon. Of course, the more I tried to explain the joke, the worse it got.

Another consequence of the terror attack was the closing of several international Muslim charities. This was due to allegations of funneling money to terrorist organizations overseas. Many of the charities didn't close because they were found guilty of funding terror. They closed because everyone was afraid to give to an international Muslim organization for fear the money would be misued and that they would be linked to possible terrorism.

Unfortunately, I know of organizations that fed orphans and refugees overseas going out of business. However, people started investing locally, which furthered a sense of American Muslim identity.

During this time, my son was a wrestler at his high school. As in many sports, the team members had nicknames for each other. My son's was "the terrorist." Before 9/11, we did not perceive this as a derogatory name.

Bullying increased in schools across the nation. Many students changed their names to sound more "American." Muhammed became "Mo." Asad asked to be called "Sammy." And Yusef became "Joe." Enrollment in Islamic schools increased as well.

A publisher wanted to publish my thesis in Lebanon, but to change the title to the "Positive Effects of 9/11 on the Muslim Community." I refused to allow the publisher to change the name. I did not want anyone to have the opportunity to misconstrue my work and keep me from returning home to America.

OKLAHOMA CENTENNIAL QUR'AN

After completing my studies, I became the full-time imam at the Islamic Society of Greater Oklahoma City (ISGOC). I hadn't lost my focus on encouraging a communal American Muslim identity. I received backlash from some members for putting the U.S. flag and the state flag of Oklahoma next to a white flag that says ISGOC on mosque grounds.

I wanted to send a message that we are not just Muslim in spite of being American. We are Americans and we are Muslim—just like a Christian may also be an American seamlessly. These identities do not conflict. We proudly raise and salute both banners.

Six years after the terrorist attacks on the Twin Towers, the state of Oklahoma celebrated its 100th anniversary of statehood. A centennial crest was placed on everything by everyone: mugs, pens, free calendars sent in the mail by insurance agents, all the kinds of swag one could imagine. Everyone was commemorating and capitalizing on this 100th-year anniversary.

I, too, wanted to show off the patriotism of my community. We had, of course, experienced hate crimes and foul language against Islam post-9/11, and had even heard some of these ignorant things spouted from our state capitol. But we really believed these things were rooted in ignorance rather than ill will.

We thought if these elected leaders actually read our holy book, they would not be so quick to say such things. Several members of our mosque and I endeavored to give each elected member of our state House and Senate a copy of the Qur'an. Some did not think this such a good idea. "We should just mind our own business and stay out of the limelight," someone said.

Muslims in America, like people from all other faiths and backgrounds, just want to live in peace. For some, the fear of drawing negative attention overrode the desire to be understood and accepted.

However, the board voted and the decision was made to go ahead with our plan. Next, we discussed which translation would be best. With much thought and discussion, we decided upon the translation by Muhammad Asad. We chose this version because Asad was a Jew who converted to Islam. His translation and commentary, I felt, would be particularly relatable to Westerners.

What really brought controversy through our halls was wanting to put the centennial seal on the Qur'ans we were to pass out. To some this seemed blasphemous, marking the Qur'an with an image. If you enter into any mosque around the world, you will find beautiful calligraphy on the walls but no pictures. Islam is starkly against idolatry, and it is blasphemous to even paint a picture of our prophet, lest his image be worshipped rather than the one true God.

To some, the centennial seal was a step toward idolatry. However, more than exploring the technicalities of tradition, I felt it important to try to meet people where they were. If a commemorative seal would make it more likely for a state representative to read the Qur'an, then I would put a seal on the Qur'an. I also wanted us to fit in more. Legislators had already received centennial Bibles as gifts. A commemorative Qur'an would sit nicely on their shelves next to their Bibles, I thought.

A group of us gathered to go to the capitol and distribute our newly minted holy book. What we thought would be an important, though somewhat innocuous, step toward strengthening ties between the Muslim community and public leadership turned into a hornet's nest. We were shocked to go to office after office and be turned away.

The narrative on Capitol Hill became that the Muslims were trying to take over and were bringing Sharia law to Oklahoma. Op-eds were written by legislators priding themselves on rejecting us and our Qur'an.

One representative, Kevin Calvey, met us at his door and said he had reservations about taking the Qur'an. Then he politely walked back into his office. He at least recognized us, we thought. Later he drafted a vehement press release, making himself out to be a hero for the state because he rejected us.

Another representative, Rex Duncan, said he did not want a copy of the Qur'an because he claimed it encourages Muslims to kill nonbelievers, women, and children.

We were quite heartbroken. Muslims believe the Qur'an was revealed to the Prophet Muhammed over a period of 21 years, and that it is the final revelation from God to humanity. Muslims all over the world have memorized the holy book, and it is considered to be virtuous to do so.

To bring someone your holy book—what you hold as most valuable— and then to be rejected, misrepresented, and hated just for bringing this gift is a very difficult thing to wrap one's mind around.

I see now how naïve we were in thinking we were honoring those politicians by gifting them with a Qur'an. Although several accepted the book, others took it to mean the complete opposite.

We were trying to communicate that there is unity in religion, especially the Abrahamic religions. We were saying, "See, we belong here." The response was essentially, "No, you are an alien, a foreigner among us. Take your book and shove it."

Though it was a difficult lesson to swallow, it created the zeal that led us to initiate an annual event: "Muslim Day at the Capitol."

STATE QUESTION 755

In 2010, there was a statewide movement to ban Sharia law from consideration in state court rulings. This initiative was, of course, spurred by some of the same lawmakers who rejected our centennial Qur'ans. The law was positioned as a preemptive measure taken to ward off the so-called threat of Sharia law taking over in Oklahoma.

It was purely a political move made by state politicians to garner strength as right-wing political leaders and to create mass hysteria. Either that, or they were woefully and fearfully ignorant of what Sharia law is—perhaps both.

The proposition was also completely worthless, as the United States Constitution already expressly denies authority to any foreign law.

On November 2, 2010, State Question 755 (SQ 755), was taken to the ballot and received support by almost 70 percent of Oklahomans. We knew this proposition to be unconstitutional, and that we could eventually get it overturned, but the real struggle was going to be trying to change the hearts and minds of those who voted in its support.

During the campaign to pass SQ 755, author Rep. Rex Duncan stated that Sharia was a "cancer" and ACT for America—a designated hate group by the Southern Poverty Law Center—had provided resources for a "media blitz," spreading fear among Oklahomans of the dangers of Sharia. The founder of ACT for America is on record for spreading hate rhetoric against Muslims, saying, "The Muslim who embraces traditional Islam but wants a peaceful coexistence with the West is effectively nonexistent."

He went further, claiming that said "peaceful Muslims" are "mythical." There was, and is, a lot of hatred to be undone.

The day the proposition passed, Muneer Awad, who was an attorney and, at the time, the executive director of CAIR's Oklahoma chapter, filed a lawsuit against the state election board. Muneer argued that should this law go into effect, we would become second-class citizens.

Muneer left Oklahoma for professional reasons, and therefore no longer had much standing in the lawsuit. I was then listed on the suit, as I had claim of constitutional injury. I was an imam at this point and, according to this proposition, I would not be able to officiate weddings or write my will according to my beliefs and wishes when I die.

SQ 755 also brought uncertainty for those persons married overseas and for those doing business overseas. The proposition didn't name any other religions. It specifically named Islam, our prophet, the Qur'an, and the Sunnah. It was rooted in fear tactics alone. It played on the general public's ignorance. The argument was that Shariah was going to supercede the law of the land—which is a legal impossibility.

It was obviously a badly written proposition and did not take long to get overturned in court. However, through the process it was no time before we started receiving death threats and experiencing vandalism and hate mail.

One person wrote on my social media page: "Take your shania law back to islam and your dessert country." I couldn't help myself; I had to reply: "Shania is a country music singer, Islam is not a country, and dessert is something you eat."

Our lawsuit was against the state election board. Our new lawyer, Michael Salan—the same one who helped me when I was being questioned by the FBI during the Murrah Building bombing—explained that we needed to nip this proposition in the bud. If incorporated into law, there would be multiple agencies we would have to sue in order to expunge the law from the books.

As we sat in court, I looked around and our side, the defendant side, was packed with hundreds of people showing up. The government's side was empty, aside from a couple of attorneys and our most oppositional state representatives, Kevin Calvey and Rex Duncan.

Judge Vicki Miles-LaGrange presided over the case. It took her 45 minutes to put an injunction on the law. I didn't know what this meant. Our attorney said, "It means we won."

When I got to the elevator after leaving the courtroom, both representatives, Calvey and Duncan, were already in it. They looked at me, then at each other, and exited the elevator. I laughed to myself, thinking about how cowardly racism really is.

After the ruling was put to rest, the Muslim community felt exonerated. We felt like the system works and that if a state agency tries to oppress us, we can go above them and find sanity at the federal level.

Oklahoma was the first state propositioning such a law, but anti-Sharia laws soon became an epidemic across the nation. They were all spearheaded by the same individual. But after our case, those proposing the laws had to change all the language that singled out Islam. They had to replace it with "foreign law" and more general language, taking the teeth out of their propositions completely.

I am not sure why this individual and his movement started in Oklahoma. Perhaps he/they thought the Oklahoma Muslim community was weak or that because our CAIR chapter was young, we would be an easy target. But through this we were able to set a precedent for the entire nation.

Many people in the West do not understand Sharia law. To them it is a conspiracy theory to overthrow governments and replace them with brutal religiosity. But Sharia law actually tells us we must obey the laws of the land we live in first, unless a law is written for the specific purpose of not allowing us to practice our faith—such as a law saying we cannot pray five times a day or that we are required to eat pork on Sundays.

These would be laws that would infringe on our ability to practice our faith and we could not follow them, but per Sharia law, we are required to follow all other laws of the land. The term "Sharia law" is somewhat of a misnomer. It's not actually a "law" at all. It's simply a set of guiding principles on how to live a moral life if you're a Muslim.

Another misconception concerning Sharia is that it is not to be imposed on anyone who does not willfully wish to observe it. Much like the Bible offers a moral code for Christians to follow, so Sharia is a moral guide for Muslims. It is a deeply personal observance. Sharia literally translates to "a path that leads to water," as it is meant to quench one's spiritual thirst.

The word Sharia in itself identifies how Islamic law is perceived. If we look at the water cycle, the water comes down from heaven as rain and is absorbed by the land and gushes out as fresh water. Thus, the interpretation of Sharia is as diverse as the Muslim community itself.

Although Islam is monotheistic, it is not monolithic. There are 1.8 billion Muslims around the world. Only five percent of Sharia law is considered to be "fixed" or non-negotiable and not open to interpretation. That is the part having to do with acts of worship: prayers, fasting, charity, etc.

What is fresh water today is not necessarily fresh in a year. So does the law evolve, much like Christian canon law or Jewish halacha.

PUBLIC DISPLAYS OF REJECTION

After several public attacks against our community, we realized our elected officials were not going to come to us. With the lawsuit still fresh in the public consciousness, we decided to go to the lawmakers and make a public statement of our resolve and resilience in the face of Islamophobia. Our community awakened to the fact that we could no longer be quiet.

We could no longer let hate speech slide. We had done that, banking on the intellectual autonomy and inherent good nature of the people of Oklahoma to dismiss false and hateful claims against our community.

But the passing of SQ 755 by such a large margin showed us our assumption and approach were wrong.

If elected officials wouldn't proactively engage with us, we would show up and engage with whoever was willing. And we would teach our children how to be civically engaged, even though we were not quite sure what that looked like.

When we established a "Muslim Day at the Capitol," it drew nation-wide coverage. We expected about 100 Muslims to show up and participate, but we did not expect the dozens of protesters who showed up as well. We knew there would be some. But there were so many and their message was so vitriolic, we began to fear for our safety.

One man's sign read, "Turn or Burn," and another: "Muhammad is dead. Jesus is not, and he has a pressure cooker for each dead Muslim." Some signs depicted our prophet in vulgar ways. Protestors spewed evil language at us as we walked past them.

I walked next to a friend of mine who is a rabbi. A man yelled at her to tell me about Jesus. She looked at him and with a bit of a laugh in her voice said, "I'm Jewish. I don't do Jesus. He does Jesus a lot more than I do." The man replied, "You're both going to hell."

As protesters, they were not supposed to come into the capitol for our event. However, some slipped past security—including a blonde-haired woman who likes to travel to Muslim events and hijack the microphone for Jesus.

We had scheduled an interfaith prayer to take place in the rotunda. As the call to prayer, also known as the *adhan*, was being made, we saw this woman try to make her way up to the podium. State troopers on security duty were able to stop her before she could cause a scene. A group of her accomplices broke out in the Lord's Prayer—as if that prayer were an offense to us.

Because of the magnitude of the protests that year and the next year, our friends in the interfaith community came to us with an idea. They would meet us at the entrance of the capitol and escort all of our families in to protect us from protests. They created what we came to call a "corridor of love" for us to walk through.

I remember seeing my friend Rabbi Jacobson, who was nearly nine-months pregnant, standing in the freezing cold to be a part of the corridor. I stopped and said to her, "I can't believe you're out here." She replied to me, "We know what hate feels like."

PARADE

Tulsa, Oklahoma has an annual Veterans Day parade every November. Many Muslims serve in the armed forces. We have veterans buried in our cemetery. It is not unusual for Muslims to serve their country. For some reason, a group of people in Tulsa thought it offensive that we participate in the parade.

It became a big controversy and, because of this, parade facilitators put our float at the end of the procession—escorted by police in armored vehicles. The interfaith community also marched with us.

There was a man dressed in an Oscar Meyer Weiner suit with a sign saying, "Muhammad is dead, Jesus is not." (We actually agree on that theologically.) When we passed by him, he would raise his hands and walk toward us, like his hotdog suit was kryptonite to us. I asked him if he wanted a hug. He did. So, I hugged him. He seemed to think I would burst into flames or convert upon skin-to-velvet contact.

Some people were instructed that when our float passed, they were to turn their backs and drop their pants. A tall man wearing jeans and a long sleeve T-shirt with the words "Allah is Satan" (which means "God is Satan") carried a bullhorn, screaming that the prophet was a pedophile and that we needed to wake up and follow Jesus Christ, along with other obscenities.

There was a barricade along the sidewalk, as there is in most parades, but for this one law enforcement was on high alert. A few times protestors broke through the barrier and the police had to come out, but thankfully this did not lead to violence. However, we did not participate in this parade again.

CHAPTER 5

Stories of Mercy

"What is the world coming to?" I said to my wife as the news flashed a story of a crazed man who attacked and beheaded a woman at a food processing plant in Moore, Oklahoma. "What?" she yelled back from another room. "Nothing," I said, not wanting to repeat the horrible story to her.

The next day I was contacted by FBI agents. They called on my cell phone, saying they wanted to talk to me about something urgent. I was preparing to leave for Washington, D.C., for the annual CAIR banquet.

"I am home," I said. "Come over; I have coffee."

They showed me a picture of an African-American man. I did not recognize him. "He attends your mosque," they said.

"There are about a thousand attendees at my mosque," I said. "If he does attend, I have never met him."

Then the agents showed me pictures posted on Facebook of this man inside my mosque with people I did recognize. "I do know those people in the pictures," I told them. They said, "This man committed a gruesome crime." After that I could be of no more service to the investigation, so they left.

The executive director of Oklahoma's CAIR (Council on American–Islamic Relations) chapter and I almost cancelled our trip to D.C. because we knew this was going to lead to many phone calls and possible threats against our community. The media tried to tie the man to our mosque and say we taught hate, bigotry, and violence.

The truth was, this man went to several different places of worship. He had been to Jewish synagogues, Buddhist temples, several churches, and our mosque. He had a Jesus Christ tattoo and another of praying hands, along with a tattoo in Arabic that read "*Assalamu Alaikum*," which translates to "Peace be with you."

He would go to different mosques during off times and pray, but would bring a Christian Bible and set it down next to him. It seemed more like Islam was the flavor of the month for this mixed-up individual. He would only speak to the African-American congregants. People in our congregation who knew him described him as "very weird."

The media reported he had converted to Islam; however, he had told people in our congregation he was a Hebrew Israelite. He had also been in jail before for assaulting a police officer.

The interfaith community planned a vigil for the families of the victims. I asked if I could go, but they decided it wasn't a good idea—considering Islam was on trial along with Alton Nolan. The heinous nature of this crime drew national attention. The media bombarded our mosque, trying to label us as a sleeper cell for terrorism.

CNN, MSNBC, Fox News, and other well-known news outlets forcefully came into our mosque and asked for statements. Fox News reporters were the most aggressive, walking through our most holy area and onto our prayer rugs without removing their shoes. Brashly standing in our sanctuary, they declared us to be terrorists. Now implicated by news outlets as the "terrorist mosque," we of course drew the attention of white supremacy groups.

Some hate websites found bird's-eye-view pictures of factory workers outside of the Vaughan Foods building, where the crime happened, wearing white robes and hair coverings. From their perspective it looked like the workers were wearing kufis, or Islamic head coverings men typically wear. They said these were Muslims praying outside as their brother was beheading the woman.

Fox News pundits Sean Hannity and Megyn Kelly, who each at the time were hosting their own shows, were looking to speak to anyone they could find to speak ill of our mosque. They eventually unearthed a white supremacist who had "converted" from white supremacy to Islam, then back to white supremacy. They blurred his face, and he told them what we were "really about."

He said we were not the same in private as we were in public and that our Friday sermons advocated violence. However, all of our sermons are archived online. Not too long after the incident, I received a phone call from someone saying they had been hired by Fox News to listen to every khutbah for diabolical messaging. They told me they took the job, but found nothing. Then they thanked us, saying they had learned a lot from watching hours and hours of our sermons.

At the same time this was happening, there was a similar beheading in Stillwater, Oklahoma, in which a white male college student, self-identifying as a Christian zealot, cut off his roommate's head. He cited witchcraft as the reason. This episode got very little media coverage.

It was Alton Nolan who was called "zealous" and, although they had both cut off the heads of another, only Nolan's case was referred to in the media as a beheading. No one came after Christianity when this college student committed this horrific crime. However, it was Islam on trial more than Nolan when he went to court.

It reminded me of the Oklahoma City coverage of my friend Ibrahim Ahmed during the Murrah Building bombing. The tone in the news completely changed once it was made public that Timothy McVeigh, a white "Christian" man, was the culprit of the attack.

The Muslim community, and my mosque specifically, were very clearly treated with bias. I personally was smeared in their crusades. In response to this religious targeting, a White House spokesperson came to our Eid dinner to read a statement from then President Barack Obama. He acknowledged our holiday of Eid and condemned Islamophobia. It was a step toward reconciliation. His presence boosted the morale of the community. In my sermon I reminded everyone how all the prophets were brothers and had come with the same message of one humanity and one compassion.

The Nolan attack was particularly hate-provoking and harmful to the Muslim community—specifically to the Oklahoma Muslim community. I received many death threats. So much so, the FBI told my family to sleep in the back room, as it was the safest in the house should someone break in or shoot at our home.

I remember walking through my house, configuring various bullet trajectories and where the best place for my family to sleep would be. It reminded me of huddling with my family in the middle of our house in Sabra and Shatila.

The Oklahoma Conference of Churches, an ecumenical and interfaith-encouraging organization, created a new interfaith award that year because of the Nolan incident, of which I was the first recipient. This meant a lot to me and my community to be recognized by our peers.

I felt what I had always known: We are not all that different. We are all just sisters and brothers of another mother.

KHALID JABARA

In 2016, the Jabara family became victims of a violent hate crime. The family had been receiving threats from their neighbor, Stanley Vernon Majors, for years. They were Orthodox Christians who had fled Lebanon in an attempted escape from religious persecution and civil war.

Just like me, they did not know the "cats" could be bigger in America. Their neighbor would yell racist obscenities at them from across the street. He would call them "Mooslems," "dirty Lebanese," and "Ay-rabs."

After having a protective order placed on the Jabaras, the threats became more violent against them. Majors threatened to kill the mother of the family.

Then one day, while walking outside and talking on the phone with her son, Rami, Haifa was struck by Majors' vehicle, leaving her for dead. Though she had several broken bones, she survived. She felt it was over: "He's done what he wanted to do." Now he will go to jail and can do nothing more, she thought.

But less than a year after being charged with assault and battery with a deadly weapon, Majors was released from jail on bail. He ended up taking a gun to the Jabara home and fatally shooting their son, Khalid.

I joined the interfaith community in going to visit the Jabara family and holding a vigil for them. I did my best to console them in Arabic. I stumbled on my words, almost speechless, unable to fathom their loss. I was again posed with the incomprehensible question of what do you say to a mother who has lost her child.

The last time I had been faced with this question was on the streets of Sabra and Shatila, hauling dead bodies away in a wheelbarrow.

Haifa had tears in her eyes as I told her I was an imam from Lebanon. I had a sense of guilt. She and her family were terrorized because they looked like me and my family. It was devastating to see that not even Christians can fit in if they look like us.

We all felt anger at the injustice done to this family, shame on the police for not protecting them from someone so blatantly violent and intent on targeting them.

I spoke mostly with the mother, although I didn't feel I had the right words. I think just being able to speak in her native tongue gave her a little bit of comfort. I did not know how to approach her family's loss from a Christian perspective, only as a Muslim.

I told her I would pray for her and her son and that his death would not be in vain. I was reminded very acutely that the relationship between Christians and Muslims in America is very different, because the ground is different.

In Lebanon we would have been enemies. Here we were each other's sources of comfort.

TERRORIST OR TERRORIZED?

The FBI called to say a white supremacist group was planning a national day of protest in which they were picketing mosques. Ours was on the list of places to which they were coming. This group often had people in the crowd who were armed.

The police were on high alert. We decided as a congregation to not shut our doors that day. We would not allow this group of radicals to terrorize us into hiding. I told my people to fight hate with love and to bring donuts for the protestors.

We had just purchased a structure adjacent to our mosque. We named it the Mercy Mission Building. I sped up its grand opening. The day the protesters arrived, and the subsequent media, I thanked them for coming and welcomed them to "the grand opening of our food pantry and free medical clinic!"

Where the media came expecting to see hate, they saw love and generosity.

Only one man had a gun. The police told me not to engage with anyone, but something about him made me walk over. He spewed hatred at me, but having grown up in a war zone, I barely noticed his rage.

I welcomed him with genuine hospitality to our new facility. He calmed down, but remained on edge. We made small talk as I inquired lightly about what he was actually protesting.

He handed me a brochure, telling me what Islam is "really" about. It just mentioned seventh-century penal law. "This would be very scary to me as well," I said.

He had a very large and conspicuous mole on his cheek. As we talked, I asked him if he had ever had it checked out. He said he had never had health insurance. "Well, today is your lucky day," I told him. He just happened to be protesting the grand opening of our free clinic.

I took his information so I could follow up with him over lunch sometime. I try to practice this often, returning hate with love and free food. Not too long afterward we did have lunch. He told me the doctor at the clinic had referred him to a specialist who also helped patients pro-bono.

The mole turned out to be cancerous and needed to be removed immediately. I was reminded of statements from state legislators, saying "Islam is a cancer," but I want people to know we are a vital organ. We are here to cure "cancer." Who would have guessed a mole would make friends of enemies?

On the morning of the protest, just as I do every morning, I opened my mail. There was a letter addressed specifically to me. This caught my attention because most of the mail—bills and such—is usually addressed to the mosque in general.

I opened my personally addressed letter and inside was a threatening message made up of clipped magazine letters, like ransom letters you see on TV. Then a white powder puffed out of the envelope. I did not want to disrupt the festivities of our grand opening, so I put the envelope back on my desk and continued to go through my mail.

The day after, I began to get concerned that the powder may have been anthrax or some other form of poison. So, I called the chief of police, Bill Citty, a friend of mine who has been a supporter of our community. He told me he would send appropriate forces. I went on about my morning. Meanwhile, the police shut down the roads for two blocks surrounding the mosque. I was not aware of all this commotion.

When the HAZMAT units showed up looking like astronauts in orange jumpsuits and breathing masks, I stopped in my tracks. "Where is the letter, sir?" one asked. "It's here," I said, as I pulled it from my inside jacket pocket.

"Sir, put that down!" the astronaut in front said. "It's been in my pocket for two days," I replied. The clipped magazine pieces shook loose and fluttered to the floor like a supremacist parade, followed by a fog of white powder covering my fingertips.

HAZMAT then "neutralized" the situation and me, giving me a shower, taking the clothes I was wearing to be tested and giving me a different set of clothes.

The powder ended up being crushed aspirin, and the letter was traced back to a man who had recently been charged with vandalizing our mosque. I'll never understand why people go through so much trouble just to show someone they hate them.

BIRD'S-EYE VIEW

I looked down from the state capitol balcony as so-called "experts" disparaged my mosque and congregants. It's a very strange thing to have a bird's-eye view of hate . . . especially when you are the one being hated, especially when you are mentioned specifically and talked about publicly as though you are not there and not human enough to acknowledge—like you are a dog and do not understand what is being said about you.

In 2016, after the legislative session, state representative John Bennett held an interim "study" on Islamic extremism. He cobbled together every Islamophobe in the country and used taxpayer dollars to bring them to Oklahoma for a bogus hearing.

If one was not aware of their agenda or knowledgeable on Islam, or lacking in acute critical thinking skills, that group's presentations would have been very convincing. They showed up with graphs and charts and Power-Points and printouts. They even brought their own vocabulary, codifying their hatred and bigotry.

Adam Soltani, the director of Oklahoma's CAIR chapter, and I sat surrounded by our interfaith allies. We sat through four hours of anti-Islam speeches, along with seeing a screen with pictures of every mosque in Oklahoma and hearing how the mosques were terrorist cells.

The Islamophobes said that every Muslim nonprofit was hiding terror-ism, that every Muslim had an ulterior motive, that we were villains trying to take over America. My Jewish friends were keenly aware at how disturbing this rhetoric was.

One "expert" was a man named John Guandolo, a former FBI agent and founder of an anti-Muslim website, understandingthethreat.com. He went on to profess that Adam's civil rights organization was really just trying to infiltrate Western civilization and destroy it from within. John Bennett then said that we and our organizations were part of a jihadi network, and that we were using relationships with other faiths as tools. He looked at my inter-faith allies and told them they were "complicit" in our subversive Muslim schemes.

At this statement my heart broke. I came expecting to be attacked, but I was not emotionally prepared for my friends to be attacked. Out of impulse, I stood up and apologized to everyone and started hugging those around me. In Islamic culture, it is not customary to hug someone of the opposite sex, but I hugged Rabbi Vered Harris and Rev. Shannon Fleck, both of whom are women.

Rabbi Harris would later make a statement that she had known me for a very long time, and had never known me to hug a female. "For him to overwhelmingly get up and start hugging everyone in the audience . . . it was a combination of rage and heartbreak communicated in a hug to everyone."

This infuriated Represntative Bennett. He requested the judiciary chair to admonish us to not hug one another. The chairman would not grant his request. This further incensed the representative, and he yelled at me to sit down.

I told him: "We no longer live on a plantation, and he's no longer the master. It's a free country." He replied, "I know. I fought for it in two wars."

Like a caged wolf, he looked up at all of the people in the balcony and, pointing, called me a "jihadi in a suit" and said that Adam and I were the top two terrorists in Oklahoma.

I looked at Adam and asked him who was number one and who was number two. He said I was older, so I was number one.

We took a selfie together and posted it on Facebook with Bennett's comment. I asked him if I should add this new title before or after my Ph.D. Bennett did not appreciate the humor and threatened to call security.

A SEAT AT THE TABLE

In the early 2000s, the Oklahoma chapter of the Dialogue Institute was established. This is an organization that seeks to promote understanding among peoples of diverse faiths and cultures.

Although there were interfaith organizations in Oklahoma already, they were primarily Christian-founded and run, mostly in reaction to the Murrah Building bombing. They did good work, but they did not know what it was like to be Muslim.

The Dialogue Institute was founded by Turkish Muslims seeking peace, and they had a unique focus on building relationships with elected leaders and those in academia. I credit them for getting us a seat at the table. Suddenly we had a friend at the police department; suddenly we knew someone in the governor's office.

Until the Dialogue Institute, we did not know what we had been missing. We started making gains in areas we did not expect.

A large segment of the more politically active Muslims in our state gathered to hold a fundraiser for then gubernatorial candidate Brad Henry. He was a very humble man, and his wife was an educator. He told us, should he become the governor of Oklahoma, he would be a governor for all people.

When he was elected, he held true to this statement.

He created advisory boards in his cabinet for minority groups. Among them was an Islamic board. Governor Henry also appointed the first Muslim to the Oklahoma Medical Board. Through the Dialogue Institute we asked him to host an interfaith Iftar dinner at the governor's mansion. This dinner marked the breaking of the fast meal during the holy month of Ramadan, when Muslims fast from sunup to sundown. It was the first time we felt welcomed.

The real surprise came during Governor Henry's reelection campaign. We told him our presence that year may hurt him politically, so we were willing to distance ourselves from him. But he looked me straight in the eye and said, "I'm the governor for all people in Oklahoma"—and left it at that. For all eight years of his term he hosted our Iftar dinner at his mansion.

However, after Governor Henry served his full term allowed by the Oklahoma state constitution, the newly elected governor, Mary Fallin, disbanded all the minority advisory boards, including ours, along with our Iftar dinner. Once again, we were ostracized and villainized by our own government. The next time a Muslim would be allowed back at the governor's mansion would be eight years later, in 2019, under Governor Stitt.

That same year, we began gaining back some ground toward equality. Our state elected a new congresswoman, Kendra Horn, and a new mayor of Oklahoma City, David Holt. Both held interfaith prayers for their inauguration, signaling they were there to represent all.

I had the privilege of leading a prayer for both. Mayor Holt's was a little different, though. A line of interfaith spiritual leaders stood to pray for the mayor. Mayor Holt's family worships at an Episcopalian church, led by Father Joseph Alsay. Unexpected by me, Father Alsay pulled out a small bottle of oil and anointed the mayor with it. I had never seen this.

This is not something Muslims do. Father Alsay said a few words in Latin and then passed the bottle to Rabbi Harris, who also put some oil on the mayor's head and said something in Hebrew. "Ok . . ." I thought. I was not prepared for this. But I took the oil and did what they did, and then said the first chapter from the Qur'an in Arabic.

This ended up being a bit of a practical joke perpetrated by Father Alsay. The mayor's name is David, and the priest was playing out the chapter in the Bible where King David is anointed by the prophet Samuel.

Jokes aside, being invited to an interfaith prayer for a mayor helped wash away the former issues we had with zoning, such as in the building of our mosque, cemeteries, schools, etc.

BOB RICKS

One of the most important relationships we cultivated over the years was with Bob Ricks. He was one of the special agents in charge during the Waco siege and then served as the special agent in charge at the FBI's Oklahoma office after the Murrah Building bombing. We began to develop a relationship with him, as the Muslim community was the first to be blamed for that act of terror.

In 2003, an Oklahoma law that made it illegal to wear a head covering when taking one's driver's license photo came to light. A 19-year-old woman in Tulsa was told to remove her hijab when she went to renew her license. She disputed this law and said it was discriminatory of women practicing Islam. Bob Ricks, who was public safety commissioner at this time, immediately issued a directive allowing for religious accommodation.

There were several other times Ricks and the Muslim community came together to make Oklahoma a safer and more inclusive place for those who lived there.

DR. KIMBALL

Islamophobia is not just a state of the heart; it is a multimillion-dollar business. I jokingly tell people that if I wanted to sell a lot of books and make loads of money, I would only have to spin a tale about some insidious Islamic conspiracy. A friend of mine, the well-respected author and professor, Dr. Charles Kimball, actually came face-to-face with such an opportunity.

He has written many books on bringing people of different faiths together. Interestingly, he was approached by a well-funded anti-Muslim organization offering him a tremendous amount of money—he did not tell me the number—to write a derogatory book on Islam.

He told them, "As a Christian Baptist minister who believes in God, I will not tell a lie about Islam and go to hell. As a professor who has written many books about bringing people together, I will not jeopardize my reputation and career. And as a human, I refuse to be anything less than my brother's keeper."

This incident inspired Dr. Kimball to write another book titled, *Truth Over Fear: Combating the Lies About Islam* (2019, WJK Press)—the exact opposite of the book he was asked to write and the exact opposite of the kind of book that can bring you wealth.

DEBORAH

Bias against the Muslim community does not just exist at the top. A friend of mine and member of my congregation, named DeBorah Bonita, runs the Mercy Food Pantry. A woman called her one day and said her daughter was incarcerated and had left her with her four children. She was desperate and out of options, not knowing where their dinner would come from.

The pantry regularly only opens on Fridays, but DeBorah told the woman she would open the pantry for her that moment. When the woman arrived, she looked around—confused at DeBorah's hijab. "I'm looking for the Catholic food pantry, Mercy," she said.

"This is Mercy Food Pantry," DeBorah told her. "We are a Muslim food pantry, but we serve everyone."

The woman narrowed her eyes, and she spat the words, "Muslim *and* Black! I'd rather starve!"

As she turned and walked back toward her van, DeBorah grabbed the four bags of groceries she had prepared and ran after her. "Please, take these groceries for your children!" she urged. The woman snarled at her.

"Please, take this," said DeBorah. The woman begrudgingly took the bags and left.

She later returned and apologized. She thanked DeBorah for insisting she take the food despite her prejudice and hateful words. That woman is now a volunteer at our food pantry.

FOOD, FAITH, AND FESTIVALS

The faith leader of St. Luke's United Methodist Church in downtown Oklahoma City wanted to engage more in interfaith work. So, he decided to throw an event to bring together the three Abrahamic religions. We were to have an opportunity to share with the others what our festivals are like, how we celebrate them, and why.

We were also to bring a food that was traditional to our faith. The Jews and the Muslims both, of course, claimed hummus as their own.

When we arrived, there were three tables set up, one for each faith. On the Methodists' table sat the biggest ham ever baked. We had a good laugh, and just as it should be, the Jews and the Muslims ate from each other's tables.

HIDING FAITH IN THE FACE OF TRAGEDY

As an imam, I receive many somber phone calls relaying news of the passing of a loved one. One phone call in particular is seared into my consciousness. Sometimes I still hear it when I prostrate for *salah*. The call came from a woman who attended our mosque.

She wasn't crying at the moment, but she had that catch in her voice that let me know she had been. "My husband is dead," she said. I told her, "My deepest condolences," then added: "*Inna lillahi wa inna ilayhi raji'un*" ("We belong to Allah and to Allah we shall return").

"He was shot 24 times," she said in a broken voice. I did not know how to respond, so I stayed silent, making space for her to speak what she needed. "You know he fought for our country," she continued. I could almost hear the tears streaming down her cheeks, but her voice stayed strong. "He struggled. I know he did."

She paused for a moment and then said: "He was found in the bushes at a trailer house, dressed in his Vietnam fatigues holding a rifle." I could hear her misplaced shame. Struggling with the mental health of a loved one is a devastating and helpless situation. I know she felt like she should have been able to prevent this tragedy.

"The police were called. When they surrounded him, my husband yelled some obscenities. He never cursed . . . except when he was having flashbacks. Then he shot at them."

I knew the rest of the story. The police opened fire on him after that. This story has no good guy or bad guy. The police were in danger, so they had to protect themselves and everyone around them. This man was not an evil person with intent to harm innocent people. He was a casualty of PTSD.

His trauma widely stemmed from a particular incident in which he saved a young Vietnamese girl. He had been in her village when the shooting began. He saw her all by herself, terrified and unable to move. He picked her up as he ran into the jungle away from the attack. They hid in the brush for days, eating whatever they could find. He protected her from incoming bombs and bullets. He held on to her like hope. She survived. He survived. But for him, survival was the only material element he escaped with.

Everything that made living not a chore had dissipated into the heat and humidity of the jungle. He hoped weakly that it rained down on the little girl and gave her joy to live a full life. He never saw her again, but he suspected she too felt like a coffee with the foam scraped off, leaving her with only bitter water in her cup.

Keeping with Muslim tradition, we brought this man's body immediately to wash. I was one of the men who washed and dressed his body. I could not count the bullet holes. The body had been autopsied, so in addition to being peppered with puncture wounds, there was a crude "Y" cut down his chest and stitched together with course thread.

The event of his death was in itself a tragedy, but what continued to break our hearts was that we had to work so hard to keep his Muslim identity a secret. He was a veteran, so he should have had a military burial. But we could just see the headlines, "Muslim convert shoots at police."

We hid his Muslim name. We cleaned his body, shrouded him, and buried him in our cemetery. We kept so quiet. The silence of those moments still haunts me today. I knew we were doing the "right" thing, but it felt like reticence had its fingers around my throat and I had to let it keep choking me.

DILEMMA

One of the greatest questions American imams must ask themselves on a regular basis is: How much do I help versus should I contact law enforcement? When someone comes to me about a friend or relative who struggles with drug issues or mental illness, it makes my heart shatter. Although other faith leaders must ask themselves the same question sometimes, as a Muslim imam I cannot make a mistake.

If someone with mental health problems is Muslim, and commits an act of violence, immediately our faith is blamed. This is not so with Christianity in America.

Shortly after the Murrah Building bombing took place, a larger-than-life statue of Jesus weeping was placed in memoriam of the victims. It's a beautiful figure. Jesus has his back turned away from the area of devastation, with hands covering his downcast face. I attended the statue's unveiling.

The perpetrator of the terrorist attack was a Christian. Not once did I look at that statue and think of him. Not once did I look at him and think his heinous actions were a reflection on his faith.

A preacher has the gift of being able to provide all resources available to help his congregants when they are suffering mentally, never worrying that if this person cannot be helped their criminal actions will put himself and his other congregants in danger of persecution.

"DIFFERENT KIND OF CATHOLIC"

Our mosque, like many churches, has a variety of services and resources we offer to individuals who show up at our door in need of help. One time a woman showed up at our mosque looking for some help to get to Texas. She said she was escaping from Arkansas, with her two children in the backseat—fleeing an abusive partner.

She had made it all the way to Oklahoma City before running out of gas. Her car rolled up on fumes into the parking lot of the Mercy Mission, the same building that houses the weekly food pantry. The building was closed, so she walked across the street to our mosque.

She told me of her dramatic exodus and asked if we could help her make it to Dallas. I took her to a nearby gas station and filled up her car. Then I asked her to come back to the mosque because I remembered seeing a stack of prefilled gas cards that could help her on her trek.

We arrived back at the mosque during one of the prayer times. This was not a midday prayer, so it was considerably less attended than during peak hours. There was, however, a steady flow of people filtering in and out of the building. The woman looked at the other men wearing kufis like me, and saw a few hijabi women with their children ambling to the doors.

"Are you a different kind of Catholic or somethin,' Father?" she asked, with brows furrowed.

I chuckled at being called "Father," then paused and said: "Yes, we are a people who believe in Jesus from the other side of the Abraham story—from the side of Ishmael."

"Oh, so Episcopal," she said. "Close enough," I replied.

FIGHTING HATE WITH LOVE

Every legislative session in Oklahoma starts the morning with a prayer led by a faith leader nominated by a member of the House. I had had the honor of leading prayer before our legislature before, but in 2017 my nomination, made by Rep. Jason Dunnington, was rejected.

When Representative Dunnington asked for clarification on why I was rejected, the conversation quickly turned into an Islamophobic rant. There was no real logical reason for alienating me, and thus the Muslim faith community, from the chaplaincy program.

In 2008, I had the privilege of leading my first prayer, of several, in the House chambers. I mentioned Jesus' name in my prayer, and afterwards several legislators came up to me and commented on how beautiful they found the prayer to be. They asked me why I would mention Jesus and wondered how mentioning his name in a Muslim prayer would not offend me.

I told them we are also people of the book. We worship the same God and believe all the prophets who came before Muhammad. We all share Abraham as the father of our religion, and sprouted from the same Mesopotamian civilization. Why would I not mention Jesus?

When my application to lead prayer was denied in 2017, I was deeply saddened. I knew the poisoned thinking that was behind it. But I did not wish to make a public stir. The optics of the legislature potentially ending the chaplaincy program and the fault falling on Muslims were not good. So, I decided to sit on it.

I chose to not make a fuss and instead to take the hit. I did, however, rather than go public, annoyed the heck out of the head of the chaplaincy program, Rep. Chuck Strohm—who also happened to be a close friend of Rep. John Bennett, who called me "Terrorist Number One." I called his office daily, though never getting through.

I visited his office as well, making it clear to his assistant that I was not necessarily looking for him to change his decision, only to give me an explanation. He never returned my calls, answered my emails, or stepped out of his office to meet me.

The next year when the legislative session began, new rules circulated through the House. Members were told they could only nominate faith leaders from their own personal places of worship for the chaplaincy program. This was a problem in Oklahoma because all of the elected leaders, at the time, were Christian or quietly practiced nothing at all.

This rule discriminated against Jewish, Bahai, Buddhist, Hindu, Muslim, and even many of the more moderate Christian denominations, and others. Now that our state was going to discriminate against not just me, but all of my interfaith friends, I could no longer stay silent and cordial.

During an annual day of interfaith prayer at the capitol, I publicly exposed this discrimination in my sermon. The media picked up the news, causing supporters to galvanize across the state.

A few weeks later, the Oklahoma Conference of Churches (OCC) held their annual day at the capitol. I always attend their capitol days because they are one of our closest interfaith allies. In a surprise move, during their keynote session, OCC's executive director, Rev. Shannon Fleck, invited all in attendance to join her in confronting Representative Strohm.

Nearly 100 interfaith allies, mostly Christian, went to the representative's office and requested to meet him. True to form, he would not come out of his office for us. Each person signed in his visitor book and wrote him a note, saying they did not approve of this discrimination.

Eventually he had to come out of his office for another meeting. Shannon Fleck pulled me into Representative Strohm's office when the door opened, before he could walk out. I was suddenly face to face with the man who discriminated against me and my faith. Seeing he had no escape without acknowledging us, he tried to shut the door to block cameras and the mob that had accumulated outside.

Shannon held the door open and said they deserved, as much as her, the right to know the meaning behind this discrimination. Representative Strohm tried very hard to wiggle out without speaking. He gave us tacit remarks about a soon-to-be-released press statement, but would give us no answers.

He whiffled through the crowd, repeating over and over, "There's a press release coming . . . there will be a statement later this week." This so-called planned press release merely doubled down on not allowing a non-Christian to perform chaplaincy duties.

Shortly after, the House speaker announced that the House would be implementing new rules, having only one appointed chaplain and no guest faith leaders. It was not a solution. My interfaith allies and I do, however, find consolation in the fact that this representative was one of the few incumbents who did not win reelection that year in his primary. The Germans have a word for this: *schadenfreude*.

The next year during that same annual interfaith prayer at the capitol, the chaplaincy policy was still slanted in a way that discriminated against all minority religions in Oklahoma. Several attorneys representing civil rights organizations came to me and told me I had a 99.99 percent chance of winning this case should I decide to sue the state.

However, with a new legislature elected and a new governor in office, I felt this was a good time to extend a hand of friendship and attempt to build bridges instead of walls.

During my sermon at that same interfaith prayer day at the capitol, I gave a message of repelling hate with love. I ended by saying to the crowd and the media present, "This is my hand of friendship reaching out to the legislature. This is my hand, extending to you Governor Stitt."

The governor heard this message, and although he did not respond immediately, he took what felt like drastic steps toward us, which his predecessor had not. He made an appearance at our Muslim Day at the Capitol—the first governor to do so. He accepted an invitation to an Iftar dinner, although his schedule later did not allow it.

These may seem like small steps, but for the Muslim community, it felt like for the first time in almost a decade we were being seen as humans rather than villains.

As a form of reconciliation, Governor Stitt set up an interfaith luncheon at the governor's mansion, which ended an eight-year ban of the Muslim community from stepping foot on the grounds. A few House representatives, including Representative Dunnington, and several faith leaders of Oklahoma's minority religions were invited. There were about 15 of us.

I was seated next to the governor. He started the conversation by going around the table and asking each of us what our community does civically and socially for the state. I, of course, mentioned our many outreach programs, including our food pantry and free medical clinic. I also mentioned that about 12 percent of doctors in the state of Oklahoma are Muslim.

When it was Representative Dunnington's turn, he addressed the elephant in the room.

"This meeting is because Imam Enchassi was denied for the chaplaincy because he is Muslim," he said. Then he went through the whole history of what had happened and how I had graciously declined to file a lawsuit.

He ended with a call for all of us, including the state government, to work together for a better Oklahoma. Everyone in the room agreed, including the governor.

GRAFFITI

It was spring semester. My class was enjoying a guest speaker, discussing the history of Christianity and elements of "extreme Christianity" such as the

KKK and white supremacy. I sat in the back of the classroom, half listening to the speaker and half grading extra-credit papers.

My phone is always on silent, but it lights up and a banner runs across the screen when I receive new messages. I saw it flash out of the corner of my eye, but I ignored it. It flashed again, then again. I glanced over and saw the word "graffiti."

The messages said the Democratic Party headquarters, less than a mile down the street from my classroom, had been vandalized with racist and hateful sayings and symbols. I asked the guest speaker to handle the rest of the remaining class time.

Graffiti is nothing new to us—"us" being the Muslim community. The mosque owns a pressure washer just for these things. So I retrieved the pressure washer and got to the headquarters as quickly as I could.

When I arrived, I saw devastating symbols of anti-Jewry and white supremacy: swastikas, the N-word, homophobic language, and death threats to leaders in the Democratic Party. It called for the decapitation of a Jewish activist in the Netherlands.

The chair of the Republican Party was there to help wash away the horribleness. She had tears in her eyes when I saw her, and she gave me a hug. I had arrived early, at about 11 o'clock. The call had been put out to the interfaith community to arrive at noon. But the vandalism was so ugly that we couldn't wait.

"Which word is most hateful?" I asked, wondering where to start. We grabbed chemicals we could find on hand to start blurring the vandalism. One woman pulled out a bottle of nail polish remover and we began muddying the hate, then power-washing it away.

MERCY

Mercy is the very soul of Islam. It is embedded throughout our holy text, flowing in and out like a thread stitching two pieces of cloth together. Of the 114 chapters in the Qur'an, 113 of them begin with the verse, "In the name of God, most gracious, most merciful . . ."

Our story of creation is one of grace. It tells of God sending the angel Gabriel to earth to bring Him a wing full of sand. God then mixed the sand of earth with the waters of heaven and blew into the lungs of His creation: mercy.

When I was young, living in the refugee camp, we were too poor to have meat every day. I remember one day a neighbor was barbequing some meat, and it smelled so delicious. My brother and I sat in the smoke, just taking it in for a moment.

When we got home, we of course still smelled like the meat. I took a piece of bread my mother had made and scratched it on my brother, and laughing said, "mmmm-mm, barbeque meat!" The next day my mother prepared some barbeque for dinner. I later learned she had skipped purchasing her drug prescription in order to buy that meat for us.

All of the mercy in the world—the mercy of a mother feeding her baby at the breast, the mercy of giving to a neighbor in need, even the mercy that animals show to each other—the Qur'an teaches that if you quantify it, this is only one percent of God's mercy.

The mercy I was shown by Ms. Rahma, walking every single day to my refugee camp, putting herself in danger just so she could save her taxi fare to buy us sugar candy; the mercy in her eyes that showed every student they were important, and made them feel as if no one else was in room; the hugs she gave to those of us who lost loved ones and the assurance she gave that she was there with us in our mourning . . .

On days when bullets were flying she was this larger-than-life umbrella, placing her body between us and the destruction outside. We knew she would take a bullet for us. Whatever was happening outside would not come inside, and if it did, she was big enough to protect us.

She would take from her own plate and give to the hungriest of us. She would tacitly say she was not hungry or thirsty so we would eat and drink. Even when she was in her 80s and suffering from Alzheimer's, she still faithfully came to the school and showed the newer teachers the beauty of her mercy.

Years ago, I was looking through my father's old papers when I found a document signed by Ms. Rahma. She had penned notes about me: "Well mannered, clean, most importantly funny."

Her full name was Samireh Abu Rahma, which literally translates to "beautiful mercy." The name Rahma means mercy, and Samireh means beautiful. She was both.

Her impact on me was so profound that when I moved to the U.S., I started a mission of mercy. From interfaith relations, to social work, to educational work and so on, all the projects I've taken on have bore the name of a Christian nun.

Oklahoma's first Islamic cemetery is named Mercy Cemetery. I started an Islamic school named Mercy School. There's the Mercy Education Foundation, Mercy Mosque, Mercy Endowment Fund, Mercy Youth Club, Mercy Chair of Islamic Studies at Oklahoma City University, and a homeless shelter named House of Mercy.

In the Mercy Mission Building we built adjacent to the mosque, we started a food panty and a soup kitchen and a medical clinic offering free medical services. We have a Mercy Sunday School program that teaches Muslim children the tenants of Islam and how to read the Qur'an.

Further, a group in Tulsa started a "Meals on Wheels" kind of program in which they deliver food to homeless communities. During the founding stages, the director called and asked if I minded if he named the project Muslims 4 Mercy. All of these ventures I've been involved in—and more—bear the name of Ms. Rahma: Mercy.

In the Qur'an, God tells the Prophet Muhammed he was sent for no other reason but to show mercy to mankind.

> *"The mission of the prophet was a mission of mercy."*
> (The Prophets 21:107)

Growing up, we survived on Christian and international welfare, which were made possible by the contributions of people from many different faiths and backgrounds. As a young boy, I never asked if the food brought to me was Muslim, Christian, or Jewish.

All I knew was it was a merciful source, and that was enough for me.

EPILOGUE

I opened my eyes to the sound of my ears popping as I felt the plane drop in altitude. We had arrived at Ben-Gurion Airport, named after the man my father feared as he fled to Lebanon. Ben-Gurion—the name of the man I had seen effigies of lit on fire and paraded through the streets of Beirut, the man responsible for the Palestinian Trail of Tears, the Columbus of Israel.

I worried about security when going through the airport, so I told the group in advance to go on without me if I was held up. But they refused. This made me a little more anxious about the whole thing. They didn't know what they were committing to.

I also had a bit of anxiety over my fellow Muslims attending the tour. I have training in interfaith relations and experience navigating uncomfortable and sensitive situations. I have made many mistakes and hurt others and been hurt by not understanding the others' perspective before speaking.

It is a common thought by those who feel deeply the pain of the Palestinian plight to see the horrors of the Holocaust and ask how anyone could go through that, then turn around and perpetrate violence on another group. But I learned very early to never compare anything to the Holocaust.

I learned to never diminish one's suffering in light of the pain of another. I just hoped all those traveling with me would be sensitive to each other.

Swimming in all of this anxiety, I realized that I was most fearful of what my emotions would be. I asked myself: How will I feel flying in to Tel Aviv, seeing the word "Israel" written over what should say "Palestine"? How will it feel to walk on the stolen streets of my grandfather?

The reason the pope and I, up until this point, had never flown into Israel via Ben-Gurion Airport is because, symbolically, it is an acknowledgment of the State of Israel—an acquiescence to the genocide of my people. Many would see this as a white flag of surrender. I feared many people back home would see it as a betrayal. For me, however, it was a flag of forgiveness—a reaching out of a hand toward humanity.

With my whole heart I am saddened by what was done to my father and grandfather, and it is important to never forget. But more than a Palestinian, more than a Muslim, I am human. I am a part of the only real race there is: the human race.

I know that despite this, the Israeli/Palestinian conflict is very close to many of my friends in my native land and in the United States. Many, like me, have close relatives or were themselves victims of highly politicized bloodshed. I cannot tell them what to do or how to fight the demons that inhabit the mind after such trauma, but this is where I am in my journey.

I arrived at Ben-Gurion Airport with priests and rabbis. I was one part of an overused set-up: "A Muslim, a Jew, and a Christian walked off a plane . . ." The reason we came is an experiment in crossing the line. Our group, "Religions United," came to listen to a different narrative than the ones we grew up hearing.

Stepping off the plane, we saw a large sign that read, "Welcome to Israel," placed in front of another sign reading "Ben-Gurion Airport." The Jewish and Christian people I came with insisted on taking a photo in front of the signs. They did not know what they were asking of me.

I could just see this picture posted on social media and all the outrage from my side of the world that would follow. I did not object, though. I took the picture.

It's a smirky picture. You can tell on my face I was uncomfortable, but also a little defiant and ready for the backlash. The reason for my trip was far more important than the grief I would receive from my friends and colleagues.

A 12-year-old Palestinian girl named Abir was shot by Israeli police after throwing a rock at them. Another girl of the same age, named Smadar, this one Jewish, was killed by a suicide bomber. Both of the girls' names translate to *fragrance*. Their parents, rather than choosing hate, decided to set up an unsanitized tour of Israel/Palestine. They wanted to facilitate the telling of a dual narrative.

We began our tour at a Holocaust museum. As I walked through the rooms, images of starved, tortured, hopeless people filled my eyes and began to leak out. Black-and-white photos of bodies mulched with rocks lined one wall. I had seen this before.

It was no different than what I saw during the massacre in Sabra and Shatila. I found myself once again towing bodies in a wheelbarrow and dumping them into a mass grave, bodies mixing in with stones. For a moment I felt the horror of that period. I found myself unable to make eye contact with the Holocaust photos.

My eyes and those pictures felt like two North Pole magnets repelling one another. Rabbi Harris, who was with me, could not even go into the museum. She waited outside for us to exit.

We were ushered to our next location. It was another museum, but this one a memorial to the children of the Holocaust. The room had bejeweled floors and floor-to-ceiling mirrors. There was complete darkness, lit by a single candle. Images of children reflected off every facet, like a diamond made of the sweetest memories.

It was so dark, you had to rely on the person in front of you and the rail to your right to proceed through the museum. There was no music, no effects. Everyone wept. I could feel everyone's thoughts, begging the same question: "How could we do this to each other?"

I was overwhelmed with sorrow for a people I was taught my whole life were my enemy.

Lunch was served graciously at the home of one Abir's parents. As we sat in their humble home, they told us the story of their daughter, of her murder by Israeli forces, and why they organized this trip for us and will continue to organize it for others. I watched the rabbis with me weep. I thought, "This is not what I 'knew' growing up."

The things we are taught as children run deep. Even now, knowing these rabbis personally as my friends, seeing them cry for the tragic death of a Palestinian child, gave me a moment of pause.

There were many moments like this throughout our visit. I experienced going to an open market right before the Sabbath, where none of the merchants would sell to the two women with us who wore headscarves. We went into a restaurant, and the host wouldn't seat us. So, we went outside the market and sat on the curb and ate sandwiches.

Two young Jewish men, on birthright to Israel, saw our mistreatment and sat down in protest next to us. Likewise, when our travels took us to Palestine, the Jewish rabbis with us were not allowed to enter the mosque. I really wanted to go in and see that ancient place of worship, but I refused to leave my friends outside.

On this trip I experienced Jews standing up for me when I lacked a seat at the table, and I stood up for them in places where they were denied respect.

It occurred to me that, had I been in Lebanon, this never would have happened. I would never have had Jewish friends. In war, there is no room for the trust needed to build relationships. And even if I somehow did have a friend of another faith, I would likely have been chastised for it.

While we were in Palestine, there was a terrorist attack on the Israeli side of the border. Rabbi Harris received a phone call from her father, checking on her safety and well-being. "I'm fine, Dad; I'm in Palestine!" she said.

One of our stops was at a Jewish settlement camp. When we arrived, our Israeli tour guide was talking to a guard who stopped our bus. Immediately he asked us what religion we were.

The guide said we were all Buddhists. My wife and I were at the front of the bus. He asked us for our identification because we looked Muslim. He was shocked at my American passport, but he eventually let us all exit the bus.

The tour guide started arguing in Hebrew with some of the settlers we were supposed to meet with. Then the language shifted to English, and we could all understand.

Our guide said, "When you came here, there were no owners? Who gave you this land?"

Settlement is a very divisive topic in Israel. There are differing viewpoints among Israelis on the right and just things to do.

"God did," the woman replied to our guide.

I couldn't keep myself from jumping in and saying, "God gave this land to the children of Abraham. Ishmael is a child of Abraham. Do you think I should come back?"

"No," was all she replied. "Palestinians," she said, "are raised to hate Jews." (This is not true, but it is not totally incorrect either. Clearly, she had also been raised to hate Palestinians.)

Growing up in a war zone does not allow your mind the freedom to see your "enemies" as fellow humans. Living in famine and fear of attack by people of another faith makes you look at your holy scriptures through a lens of hate.

Furthermore, if you are uneducated and lack the ability to read sacred texts yourself, you can only "know" what is being taught from the pulpit. These preachers are often not ill-intended; rather, they only have a lens of pain with which to look through, and they too are often uneducated.

As I grew in my faith, I relearned scripture in a safe environment without war and without name-calling, and discovered that friendship and love between all people is exactly what the Qur'an calls for. There are many verses in the Qur'an discussing *ahl-alkitab*—people of the book—Jews and

Christians who received scripture before us. Many verses mandate us to not debate with them, but rather to dialogue.

Do not debate with the people of the book except in the best possible manner; rather dialogue in the best possible manner. (Qur'an 29:36)

It is a sacred and beautiful privilege to be able to sit across from someone who sees God a different way and say, "I do not agree with you, but this does not mean we must be enemies."

After our trip, as I boarded the plane and watched the Ben-Gurion Airport diminish in the horizon behind me, I thought of all the borders I have crossed—the wars fought between them and the people caught in the middle.

I thought of the lessons I have learned from crossing these lines, how there are three things needed to find peace among religions:

1. **E**ducation
2. **A**ttitude
3. **R**elationships

"Lend me your EAR" is how I thought I would start out my next semester's class on interfaith and religious pluralism.

As an educator, my work has been twofold. The first is through interfaith efforts shared with others. We have produced public service announcements advocating for education, including once when some imams were arrested at an airport for praying.

Two fellow educators and I did an interfaith tour of Oklahoma. Dr. Charles Kimball, chair of religious studies at Oklahoma University, who is a Baptist minister of Jewish roots, with a Ph.D. in Islamic studies, and the Rev. Dr. William Tabbernee, then the executive director of the Oklahoma Conference of Churches who taught at Phillips Theological Seminary, joined me in speaking in churches, synagogues, civic centers, and anywhere anyone would listen.

We called listeners to learn about other religions from the sources, from the actual practitioners of the faith. Dr. Tabbernee liked to mention the "Three C's" of interfaith work. He would say it's about "conversation," not conversion; "communication," not confrontation; and "cooperation," not condemnation.

I have had the opportunity to be the first Muslim speaker at a couple of universities in Oklahoma. I was on a panel discussion with the well-known author and director of the Yale Center for Faith and Culture, Dr. Miroslav Volf. The topic of this discussion was, "Do Muslims and Christians worship the same God?"

An audience member stood up and said Muslims do not worship the same Judeo-Christian God because Muslims do not have the concept of the Trinity. I said, "I guess Jews and Christians don't worship the same God either, then." His bias was immediately revealed, and I think it provided everyone an opportunity to reflect on their own.

A rabbi and I went to a Baptist university to speak to a class. While waiting, we took a look at their textbooks and realized very quickly they were more propaganda than educational. We spoke to the professor and, through relationship and time, were able to get them accurate textbooks.

After that I found myself leading workshops and addressing common misconceptions. I shared that *Jihad* means "to strive"—not "holy war." In Islam, women are to be respected and revered. Shariah law is not about killing people. Islamic civilization has been incredibly valuable to the human race in that we invented algebra, made many scientific advances, and even came up with coffee. (Where would America be without coffee?)

The second side of my educational work is in training my own people. As an imam, I want my congregation to understand the importance of inter-faith work. I want to show them how by doing this work we are adhering to the tenants of our faith; that we don't do interfaith work despite our faith, but because of it.

This has been a harder sell than talking to non-Muslims about Islam. It's like trying to teach your own family something. It's often more difficult than with strangers.

The Muslim community is also incredibly diverse, which brings its own barriers to overcome. The mosque I serve has more than 72 ethnicities from 40-plus countries, each having its own culture and politics to navigate.

Education has the power to change one's attitude. Every time a terrorist attack happens, I instruct my congregation that their first prayer should not be, "God, don't let them be Muslim." It should be, "God help the victims who are dealing with this tragedy."

I try to teach that our faith is not just about a long beard and a robe, but about feeding the hungry, caring for the orphan, helping our neighbors, and engaging in conversation around social issues. I encourage my fellow brothers and sisters to meet their elected leaders and to vote.

We must have the right attitude to make peace. Attitude affects the way we live and how we serve one another.

Every year, when teaching my classes, I assign my students a service project with a learning component. I tell them to pick an organization they are afraid of or lack understanding in.

"Everyone has a racist Uncle Bob," I tell them. "You know who your 'Uncle Bob' is. He's the relative who wants to talk politics over Thanksgiving dinner."

It isn't he who I am concerned with, though, I tell them. Uncle Bob wants to convince you that America is doomed because of a certain group or class of people in this country. "That's the group I want you to serve with this semester!"

I want to instill a new attitude in my students by providing the opportunity for them to receive an education firsthand from someone they know little to nothing about. At the end of the semester each student gives a presentation on his or her service project.

The most memorable one came from a young woman in my class who chose to serve in a Jewish synagogue. She was there the day the Pittsburg shooting happened in 2018. She was sitting in the service when the rabbi received three calls in a row on her phone—which seemed to be some kind of coded message for an emergency.

"We have a code red," the rabbi said to the congregation. The rabbi immediately instructed security to shut the doors. My student said she had never felt so scared in her life.

"Why would someone be that hateful?" she asked. "Why would you shoot someone because of their religion?"

The whole class was tearful. I was tearful. Many attitudes in that classroom were changed that day. Many students gained a deeper understanding of what hate and love look like.

Most importantly, both education and attitude are sealed through relationship. It was through relationships with Ms. Rahma and Ms. Ghalia that I knew not to hate Christians when a sect of them raided and murdered my entire city. It was through relationships that I learned Jews are not my natural-born enemies.

We all have privilege somehow. I had a congregant member who had recently converted to Islam. He was a very fair-skinned man with red hair and blue eyes. He had fallen in love with a Muslim Lebanese girl and wanted to ask her parents in Lebanon for her hand in marriage. I offered to go with him.

Together, we flew to Lebanon. When we left America, he was the one with privilege. I was brown-skinned, and English was my second language. But when we landed in Lebanon, suddenly the tables were flipped. He was the outsider.

He looked at me, overwhelmed by the mass of people, and asked: "How can I blend in?" I looked him up and down and said, "Dude, you can't. But I'm here to help you."

I used my brown Muslim privilege to help him navigate the system and made him aware of cultural proprieties regarding marriage, and within a week he was married.

In Jerusalem, my fellow Jewish travelers stood up for me when certain merchants wouldn't sell to me. I stood up for them when we crossed over to Palestine and certain mosques wouldn't let them enter.

It is powerful for me in places where Islam is the majority to stand up for the rights of my Christian and Jewish brothers and sisters. And it is powerful for them to stand up for mine.

I take every opportunity to teach others about my faith. When asked to lead prayers for mixed groups, my prayers focus on shining light on our commonalities.

On the flight home from Ben-Gurion Airport, I fine-tuned an interfaith prayer I use when leading prayers for the state legislature. This is the prayer I will use when given the next opportunity:

> **Lord of Adam and Eve:** You created us from a single Soul (that of Adam and Eve) and made us into tribes and nations so we may know one another, serve one another, and aid one another . . . Make us worship you today, Lord, by servicing your creation equally. Make us not deviate from the path of Paradise again. Make us see one another as children of Adam and Eve. And grant us to see that racism, bigotry, and injustices are evil products of the forbidden tree.
>
> **Lord of Noah:** Guide us to understand that although we might have come on different arks, that we might have crossed different

oceans, help us realize that we are now together in the promised land. We all pray to Almighty God to guide all of us to a world where we no longer cower in its darkest corners, shivering from the fear of one another.

Lord of Abraham, Ishmael, Isaac, and Jacob and the tribes: We pray that God Almighty make our nation a place of peace without atrocities, brutality, homicide, and horror.

Lord of Joseph: Open our hearts and minds to hear your voice, speaking peace, tolerance, and love. Help us to learn forgiveness, kindness, and to have open minds and hearts. Help us, Lord, to search deep within our souls so we may hear, feel, and touch the divine harmony of your love. Assist us to forgive those who have wronged us, to pardon those who have oppressed us, and to support those who have forsaken us.

Lord of Job: Grant us patience, endurance, and tolerance. Lord, you are the fountain of everlasting peace and healing balm. Just as you washed Job of his sickness, wash over our families and societal wounds of hatred, intolerance, and war. Scrub away the deep stains that destroy the fabric of our country.

Lord of David: Help us search deep within our souls so we may hear, feel, and touch the divine harmony of Your love, wisdom, and justice.

Lord of Moses and Aaron: Help us stand side by side as brothers and sisters, fearlessly against injustices, for indeed we know that if we stand up for justice You, Lord, will be with us. We know that we are never alone if You are with us. Lord, we are not praying for You to drown our pharaohs of this world, rather to keep them afloat so they can find their way back to You.

Lord of the Messiah Jesus Christ and Virgin Mary: We pray that the Almighty guides us to a unified world, a unified state, and a unified city of our own Jerusalem—the city of God among the red clay of our land. Help us feed the hungry, house the homeless, and cure the sick.

Lord of Muhammed: You sheltered him as an orphan, so he decided to adopt the world. Help us to promote social justice. Assist us to support public welfare, and grant us the will and the determination to look after the elderly and to respect the young. Help us today to assist those who are less fortunate around the world.

Lord of Justice: Who desires us to do justice, love mercy, and walk humbly with You, we thank You for inspiring us with the life and example of those who have come before us. Grant us the wisdom to truly understand that all of humanity is created equally. Console us with this wisdom, comfort us by following this wisdom, and aid us to follow it in all of our daily practices. We come together today so our prayers will be uplifted to shine the way to the kingdom of heaven. We ask you, Lord, to answer our prayers, in your divine, merciful, compassionate name. Amen.

My family table is a representation of the world. I am an American, Egyptian, Palestinian, Syrian, immigrant, and refugee. My wife sits next to me with Mexican and Native American blood running through her veins. Our children and in-laws are all of the above and more.

My daughter when applying to college asked me, "Dad, what are we? Do I put Native American, Hispanic, Black, Caucasian . . . ?" "Yes," I said. "Pick the one that's going to give you the scholarship."

At Thanksgiving we talk about the trail of tears, slavery, immigration, and Islamophobia. One celebrates, while the other mourns. Some recognize Columbus Day; the others call it Indigenous People's day. Our turkey is basted in enchilada sauce, wrapped in tobacco leaves, stuffed with garbanzo beans, and deep fried in olive oil, served on a bed of rice.

We laugh, and eat. We cry, and we pray together, because we are family; and we all have a seat at the table..

In this compelling and hopeful book, Imad Enchassi chronicles his remarkable journey from a Palestinian refugee camp in Beirut to American citizenship and his vocation as the leading Imam in his adopted home state of Oklahoma. A tireless educator and activist, Enchassi not only models interfaith understanding and cooperation, but he also inspires people of faith and goodwill to join in the urgent work for a healthier future in our all-too-quarrelsome human communities. Read *Cloud Miles* and you will want to share many of the heartwarming and humorous stories. Give this wonderful book to your family and friends. I guarantee they will thank you!

The Rev. Dr. Charles Kimball
Presidential Professor
Chair of Religious Studies
University of Oklahoma

Cloud Miles is testament to the power of love, justice, and mercy. Imad Enchassi's stories will break your heart again and again as he describes the hate he and his community have experienced throughout his life. But his commitment to his fellow humans, the humanity of all people, and interfaith engagement will warm your heart, and shows that even the deepest wounds and most bitter hate can be overcome with a power much stronger: love.

Sharon Betsworth
Professor of Religion
Director, Wimberly School of Religion
Oklahoma City University

Imam Enchassi has been a champion of engagement and dialogue throughout his life and ministry. In *Cloud Miles,* one can see the roots of such passion and drive to make the world a better place. Through the intimacy in which Enchassi tells his story, the reader is brought alongside a man who endured life's extreme prejudice and hatred, and emerged committed to love and unity. We are also welcomed into a conversation regarding the immense discrimination and hatred put upon a faithful people and how that plays out for Muslims in the United States. This book is a vital read, both in understanding the endurance of compassion and love, and to continue growing as people who are called into the immense welcome of all.

Shannon Fleck
Executive Director
Oklahoma Conference of Churches

Despite living in a world that regularly directs violence not only at those in his faith background but also squarely at those in his own nuclear family, Imad Enchassi is a remarkably cheerful and compassionate leader for interfaith understanding.

Until you learn someone's story, you never really know what makes them who they are. *Cloud Miles* gets to the core of who he is and tells the beautiful and humanizing story of where he came from.

It's been suggested that those seeking to expand their empathy will benefit by gaining direct experience of other people's lives, putting into practice the proverb, "Walk a mile in another man's moccasins before you criticize him." In reading *Cloud Miles*, one will gain fresh empathy by experiencing the remarkable miles traveled by a refugee who received, and generously shares, the gifts of mercy, peace, and purpose on the journey.

With wit and wisdom, he teaches urgent lessons about the dangerous consequences of unchecked hate. I encourage anyone who is trying to find hope and a way forward in a world that is increasingly divided to read the imam's story. It is a testament to the enduring power that love has to overcome the forces of evil.

Respect for others who are different than us should be an integral part of our faith. Listening and reading through the lenses of another enhances our sensitivity, compassion, and most importantly, our relationship with God.

Dr. Bob Long
Senior Pastor, St. Luke's United Methodist Church
Oklahoma City, Okla.

The poet William Wordsworth once said, "The child is father of the man." My friend and colleague Imad Enchassi is living proof that what happens to us as children shapes everything about the adults we become.

Now he has decided to share his journey with us in this amazing book. He walks us through his life, from war-torn Lebanon where he witnessed both the heroic and horrible, to his arrival in America, to his leadership of the Oklahoma Muslim community in one of the most homophobic places on earth.

Through it all, he finds the best in other people, and makes us laugh at the same time. If you want to feel better about the human spirit, and truly understand the faith of our Muslim sisters and brothers, then read this book, and then get to know your neighbors. Nothing would please my favorite imam more.

Rev. Robin R. Meyers, Ph.D.
Senior Minister, Mayflower Congregational UCC Church, Oklahoma City
Distinguished Professor of Social Justice Emeritus, Oklahoma City University

Cloud Miles reflects the work of building not only religious community, but also community spirit. It matches my dear friend Imad Enchassi's presentation of selflessly being involved in trying to help all of us come together in understanding our purpose of loving and living together. It is a natural outgrowth of what he has been living, and his purpose has touched so many lives. My prayer is that many will read this book and feel his presence and will be moved by the work he is doing to make our world better.

George Young
Oklahoma State Senator

This is a beautiful book—one of the most moving memoirs of interfaith leadership that I have ever read. It deserves a wide audience. May it help all of us live up to the ethic of mercy and pluralism at the heart of both America and Islam.

Eboo Patel
Founder and President, Interfaith Youth Core
Author, Out of Many Faiths

In *Cloud Miles*, Dr. Imam Imad Enchassi opens his heroic life's global journey as a Palestinian refugee to his riveted readers.
Through this engaging commentary, we are present at the defining, often perilous moments in his self-discovery amid the myriad, life-changing events and circumstances beyond his control.

These realities, including the swirl of the turbulent history of the Middle East and the Palestine-Israeli conflict, have contoured his life. Imad offers responses that emanate from the heart and that are grounded in peace building.

Imad is an archetype of the interfaith leader despite the challenges of bridging cultural differences. In this highly readable personal story, we find testimony to Imad's prescription for peace—namely education, attitude, and relationships.

Despite the cascading threats and hardships that could be used to justify enmity and bitterness, Imad models another way: to reach out to those who would vilify you because you seem different, and to embrace the values and hopes that bind us in the human family.

I enthusiastically recommend *Cloud Miles*.

Don Betz, Ph.D.
President Emeritus
University of Central Oklahoma

If you only read one new book this year, make it *Cloud Miles*! You'll be captivated by Imad Enchassi's poignant journey from refugee in war-torn Lebanon to becoming imam of the Islamic Society of Greater Oklahoma City, USA.

You will also gain invaluable insights into the geographic, political, and religious context of the Palestinian/Israeli conflict from someone whose family was evicted from their own country by Jewish Zionists and whose relatives and friends were later slaughtered by Maronite Christians.

Cloud Miles is a real-life story of personal courage, true heroism, and deep faith lived out under extremely difficult circumstances in the Middle East. It is also the account of a Muslim immigrant who, on April 19, 1995, was suspected by the FBI of being "John Doe No. 2" in the Alfred P. Murrah Federal Building bombing in Oklahoma City and who, like so many other American Muslims, has been the target of hate crimes, especially after September 11, 2001.

Cloud Miles provides a much-needed corrective to the frequently erroneous and bigoted portrayal of Islam in America. Imam Enchassi illustrates through countless examples how the Islamic faith is lived out by patriotic and loyal citizens of the United States. He also demonstrates the contributions Muslims make to their local communities and to the country as a whole as well as the way mainstream Muslims engage positively with people of other faiths.

Rev. Dr. William Tabbernee
Executive Director Emeritus
Oklahoma Conference of Churches

History is too important to leave its telling to the history makers. It must be told by individuals who find themselves caught in the middle of it—those who suffer its consequences; those who enjoy its benefits; those who live on the ground.

Imad Enchassi writes his story as a refugee who only by God's will survives a massacre, as a member of the huddled masses who finds freedom, as a sleep-deprived soul who snatches the American dream, and as a foot soldier who battles for tolerance. This is a story of a downtrodden man responding to his oppressors with the most unusual gifts—peace, mercy, and humor.

Rev. Andrew Tevington
Retired United Methodist Pastor

Dr. Enchassi shares his important story with skill—at once riveting and compelling, often deeply troubling, and always imminently hopeful. This is a tale of crossed boundaries, a tale of the convergence of diversity and the beautiful embrace of complexity.

It is a profoundly "American" story—understanding and embracing, hopeful and confident—for a time in which we must resist the rise of hatred and fear. It is my prayer, God willing, that you'll read this story and be inspired to generate your own compassion and generosity, where you are and with what you have.

Rev. Chris Moore
Senior Minister, Fellowship Congregational United Church of Christ
Tulsa, Okla.

Imad Enchassi is one of the most remarkable people I have ever known. He lights up the room as he enters, and he genuinely connects with everyone he meets. I first saw him at an interfaith community activity in Oklahoma City many years ago. Our friendship has continued to develop, and I now give annual lectures on Buddhism to his university religion classes.

His continuing efforts to build peace have not only made Oklahoma a better place to live, but also have reached out to a struggling world and soothed it by establishing caring connections with others. I am very happy that he has chosen to share his life experience in the pages of this book. When you read it, you will feel that he has lived many lifetimes within this short time on earth.

He is a full-spectrum human being—full of deep compassion, profound wisdom, and delightful humor. I am so grateful our paths crossed.

Rev. Kris Ladusau
RK Buddhist Dharma Center of Oklahoma

I am deeply appreciative of Imam Enchassi's tireless efforts to seek common purpose and set aside the things that too often divide us. Enchassi has a gift for reminding us of our shared humanity. Empathy and love are the surest paths to coexistence in this world, and I admire his commitment to these ideals.

David M. Holt
Mayor of Oklahoma City, Okla.

Cloud Miles details the magnificent pilgrimage of a remarkable man. From Imad Enchassi's humble beginnings in Lebanon to becoming one of the world's great ambassadors for interfaith work, *Cloud Miles* invites readers on a journey of heartache, mercy, and hope. For anyone interested in a peaceful future and unrestrained hope, read this book today.

Rev. R. Mitch Randall, D.Min.
Executive Director, Good Faith Media

Some people give hand-arranged flowers to a very sick friend; others, a carton of medjool dates to a fellow pilgrim in need of encouragement. A few do-gooders are blessed with the gift of speech and voice, and can move crowds of people to do acts of kindness. All of these techniques and gifts and many more are in Imad Enchassi's tool kit. Perhaps the top leader of interfaith dialogue in Oklahoma City, it is difficult to imagine our city and state without him. His story is a great and inspiring read.

Judge Robert Henery
Former U.S. Circuit Judge
Former Attorney General of Oklahoma
Retired President, Oklahoma City University

Imam Imad Enchassi, Ph.D., is a senior imam at the Islamic Society of Greater Oklahoma City, the Chair of Islamic Studies at Oklahoma City University, and a visiting professor at Phillips Theological Seminary and Saint Paul School of Theology. Dr. Enchassi has received many interfaith, community, diversity and inclusion awards, and has been featured in media outlets including CNN, MSNBC, ABC, Al Jazeera, and Al Arabia. In 2020, *The Daily Oklahoman* named him a "Visionary in Religious and Education Outreach." He is a founder of several educational, social, religious, and charitable organizations including Mercy Mission. His passion for peace and compassion stems from his upbringing in war zones and surviving the 1982 Sabra and Shatila Massacre.

CPSIA information can be obtained
at www.ICGtesting.com
Printed in the USA
LVHW041526230320
650911LV00020B/2864

9 781635 280906